Quarterly Essay

Quarterly Essay is published four times a year by Black Inc., an imprint of Schwartz Books Pty Ltd. Publisher: Morry Schwartz.

ISBN 9781760644215 ISSN 1444-884x

Subscriptions – 1 year print & digital (4 issues): $89.99 within Australia incl. GST. Outside Australia $134.99. 2 years print & digital (8 issues): $169.99 within Australia incl. GST. 1 year digital only: $59.99.

Payment may be made by Mastercard or Visa, or by cheque made out to Schwartz Books. Payment includes postage and handling.

To subscribe, fill out and post the subscription card or form inside this issue, or subscribe online:

quarterlyessay.com
subscribe@quarterlyessay.com
Phone: 61 3 9486 0288

Correspondence should be addressed to:

The Editor, Quarterly Essay
22–24 Northumberland Street
Collingwood VIC 3066 Australia
Phone: 61 3 9486 0288 / Fax: 61 3 9011 6106
Email: quarterlyessay@blackincbooks.com

Editor: Chris Feik. Management: Elisabeth Young. Publicity: Anna Lensky. Design: Guy Mirabella. Associate Editor: Kirstie Innes-Will. Production Coordinator: Marilyn de Castro. Typesetting: Typography Studio.

Printed in Australia by McPherson's Printing Group. The paper used to produce this book comes from wood grown in sustainable forests.

VOICE OF REASON

On Recognition and Renewal

Megan Davis

WE HAVE NEVER MET

I am a quintessential '80s kid. At family functions in Brisbane, I sit with my siblings, all of us in our forties, searching YouTube for the intro themes to our favourite kids shows: *Adventures of the Gummi Bears, Roger Ramjet, Bananaman, Mighty Mouse, Chocky* and *The Banana Splits*. And besides the US and British influence, we search for the iconic Australian TV programs of our youth: *The Nargun and the Stars, The Henderson Kids* and *Secret Valley*. Of course, for any kid of the '80s, there was also John Farnham. If *Whispering Jack* was the soundtrack to our youth, the soundtrack to the first referendum campaign in the era of social media, dominated by Trumpian misinformation, must be Farnham's *Age of Reason*.

The most common question from Aussies since the Uluṟu Statement from the Heart was read out to the Australian people – after, What question is on the ballot paper? – is: Why don't you ask Johnny Farnham if he will let you use his song for the campaign? or, Have you thought of Farnham's "You're the Voice"?

Written after an anti-nuclear protest in Hyde Park, it is a song for the ages. A song that Farnham himself has said is an anthem for all Australians. The song has us looking at one another down a gun-barrel. But it also urges us to turn the page over. In Grade 6, I choreographed a dance to it in the back room of Mum's housing commission home in Eagleby with my mate Clare

Rapkins. For me, the song spoke of action, momentum, agency and the power of voice, but more importantly about finding ways to move forward even when there's disagreement and tension, not letting the past be a burden on the future. And here we are in 2023, staring down the barrel of a gun. I use that phrase metaphorically.

The polling for the Voice to Parliament over the six years since the Uluṟu Statement tells us there is a fair chance of winning a referendum vote. We have solid support. Unlike at the failed republic referendum of 1999, when the majority population in every major city was Australian-born, in 2023 our capital cities are filled with the overseas-born or those with migrant parents. The demographics have changed, the politics have changed. Attitudes towards Aboriginal and Torres Strait Islander Australians have changed too. Aboriginal culture is more present and more visible. Year after year, more young Australians learn about Aboriginal culture in kindergarten, primary school and high school.

Even so, Noel Pearson described Aboriginal people in his 2022 Boyer Lectures as the "most unloved people" in Australia. This caused some angst among the pundits. The Apology to the Stolen Generations, the Reconciliation Action Plans (RAPs), the ubiquitous Acknowledgements of Country and the national anthem sung in Language: were these not the gestures of a loving nation? Surely this epithet, "the most unloved," was better applied to the protection era or the invective of the post-Mabo time?

Pearson's theory will be tested in 2023, as we enter the final stretch leading to the referendum. The 2023 poll is the culmination of a twelve-year project that commenced with Prime Minister Julia Gillard's Expert Panel on Constitutional Recognition of Indigenous Australians. Since 2011, we have had seven public processes, including two parliamentary committees and a referendum council, and ten public reports on the one topic: constitutional recognition for Aboriginal and Torres Strait Islander peoples. That is a lot of public policy work in plain view.

The form of recognition proposed is a constitutionally enshrined Aboriginal and Torres Strait Islander Voice to the Parliament. This proposal evolved from twelve deliberative dialogues conducted across Australia and involving a robust sample of First Nations communities (remember that First Nations are collectives, not individuals). The results of the deliberation were not handed to the prime minister in a ritual ceremony, as is customary, but rather issued to the Australian people as an "invitation." The Uluṟu Statement from the Heart appealed to Australians to "walk with us in a movement of the Australian people for a better future."

At first glance, this seems more a Pollyanna sentiment than hard-edged law reform, but the delegates who attended the regional dialogues and then the national convention at Uluṟu believed a different strategy was required than the ritual issuing of petitions to governments or parliaments that rarely implement them. It was agreed that politicians have too much self-interest and this pledge needed to engage Australians on a higher level than political cynicism. The heart and the head. People, not politicians.

In the dialogues, people recalled the many petitions made over the decades to political leaders, only for them to be dismissed as soon as the government jet's wheels lifted from the tarmac. They recalled those seminal statements and earlier petitions preserved behind glass and wheeled out for NAIDOC Week or National Reconciliation Week by the Australian parliament. Like the Aboriginal flag, they all inevitably become the property – or enter the custody – of the Commonwealth.

During the closing ceremony of the National Constitutional Convention in 2017, we were adamant that the "gifts" – the Piti, Tjutinypa and Tjara – handed to us by Pitjantjatjara elder Sammy Wilson, a traditional owner of Uluṟu, on behalf of the Mutitjulu community, would not fall prey to the national ritual of fawning over tangible objects while eschewing the substantive ask. This is why the Uluṟu painting from the national convention was taken out of circulation five years ago. The Piti (bowl), Sammy Wilson explained, was to carry the message across Australia. Of the Tjutinypa (club and chisel), he said, "That's the weapon you use to keep talking with the politicians." The Tjara (shield), he said, was "to defend the Uluru Statement and to keep the message straight."

When I flew to Canberra following the Uluru Statement in May 2017, along with Noel Pearson, Pat Anderson and Sally Scales, for an ABC TV broadcast of *Q&A* from Parliament House, we entered the Great Hall to take our seats on the set. Inauspiciously, beside the doorway was a box displaying the Barunga Statement. Would this also be the fate of the Uluru Statement from the Heart? To become one in a long line of serious and substantive proposals for structural change refashioned into an historical artefact by the Frozen Continent?

Changing the constitution is a mammoth task. During the regional dialogues, I would recite the record with some trepidation: only eight out of forty-four referendums have been successful since 1901. The old people would chortle knowingly, for they remembered the 1967 referendum, when Australians voted "Yes" to the federal power to make laws for Aboriginal people. They had either been active in the campaign themselves or watched their parents campaign. They were not deterred by the record. They would proudly declare they had received the highest "Yes" vote in the history of Australian referendums. They were earnest in their faith in the fundamental decency of the Australian people. The 2023 referendum campaign will determine whether that faith is misplaced or not.

The story so far seems to suggest that Pearson's theory of the "most unloved people" belongs to an Old Australia. This Ghost of Australia Past is sustained by a cashed-up "No" campaign, reliant on the economic and social might of the conservative silent generation and baby boomers, with in-kind support from some media. Conservatives are busy carving out a convenient narrative for themselves that there is a reasoned and respectable case for "No"; there isn't. As journalist Niki Savva wrote recently, "While it is not true to say that every Australian who votes No in the Voice referendum is a racist, you can bet your bottom dollar that every racist will vote No." The cumulative wealth and power of the rusted-on "No" voters, their prominence in media ownership and on corporate boards, their conservatism and their unwillingness to commit to social change should be juxtaposed with the ascendant, vibrant, new Australia, one that believes in social change and inclusion.

New Australia appears to form the rump of the consistent majority "Yes" polling over the past six years. It includes gen Z and millennials, our multicultural brothers and sisters from the Middle East, North Africa and South Asia, and followers of Islam, Buddhism, Hinduism and the Greek Orthodox and Catholic faiths. It involves people with low incomes who live in the working-class areas that are the heavy lifters of multiculturalism and social cohesion in this nation. These Australians have thought about it and believe the Voice will improve government decision-making about the lives of Aboriginal and Torres Strait Islander peoples, and therefore will make Australia a more inclusive country.

The last election saw the consolidation of this New Australia. Australians voted in droves for the Greens and for "Teal" independents in previously safe Liberal seats. This demonstrated a groundswell of sentiment for action on federal corruption, climate change and the Uluṟu Statement from the Heart. This movement of the Australian people was missed by the Canberra commentariat. And while other liberal democracies, such as France, have seen the hollowing-out of the socialists and the liberals fuel the extreme left and right, in Australia we have seen a discernible shift to the centre-left (and the plummeting of the primary vote of both major political parties). Driving this seismic shift is a voter base that is sick and tired of the bickering of the major parties and the concomitant inertia on change: on fixing the things that matter to Australians.

On the Uluṟu Statement from the Heart and a constitutional Voice to Parliament, Australians could see an unconventional yet compelling invitation to address one of the most acute challenges for Indigenous Australia: *getting the government to listen*. Persuading the nation of the exigency of change draws on Australians' observation that the status quo for Aboriginal and Torres Strait Islander peoples is not working, and their own experience of bureaucracy as mean-spirited and punitive, as hundreds of thousands of Australians experienced firsthand with the Robodebt scheme.

Australians have low levels of trust in their politicians, seeing them as too absorbed by adversarial parliamentary politics, internal leadership quarrels and internecine pre-selection spats. Seminal to this is the failure of Canberra to hear Australians in times of need. The spectre of a prime minister, Scott Morrison, abandoning his people in their darkest hour, amid fire and flood. Together, we have been let down as a people. This is a unifying sentiment.

The invitation issued to the Australian people is also shadowed by the three-decades-long reconciliation process that began after Prime Minister Bob Hawke reneged on his commitment to a treaty at Barunga in 1988. Instead of a treaty – because a Western Australian election was looming and the electoral calculus of Aboriginal recognition and mining interests did not mesh – Hawke's cabinet decided a reconciliation process was needed first. "Reconciliation" was the fad of the '90s. Developed in Latin American countries and in South Africa, it purported to bring societies back together after serious conflict or dictatorship, in a process known today as "transitional justice." It theorised a pathway for perpetrators and victims to reconcile and live together in peace under the rule of law. Transitional justice has failed many of the countries that deployed it (and there are *many*, given it has the United Nations' stamp of approval). In the dialogues, our old people kept saying, without prompting, that "reconciliation" was the wrong word. They said it implied the restoration of friendly relations after a conflict, but, they said, *we have never met*.

This is what the Uluṟu Statement stands for. It is a beginning. It is about recognition, and it is about renewal. It is a hand of friendship extended to the Australian people, an invitation to come and meet with us. In issuing the statement to all Australians, the First Nations hope to bypass the ritual cynicism of Australian retail politics and ask Australians of all religions, cultures and political persuasions to read the Uluṟu Statement and hear, in our own words, the logic for change:

> We seek constitutional reforms to empower our people and take a rightful place in our own country.
>
> We call for the establishment of a First Nations Voice enshrined in the Constitution.

We hoped Australians would listen. And they were listening. They are still listening. Thus, we have a commitment to a referendum, a clear roadmap of reform, a twelve-year recognition process debated by successive governments and parliaments, an alteration to the text and a ballot question. For this referendum to succeed will be a monumental achievement of this nation. But we are not there yet. To arrive at our destination, we need to explain to Australians why the Voice is needed. Indigenous policy issues are alien to most and the loudest voices on the subject are often the politicians who were most ineffective in this policy area.

To begin that work, I want to share a famous Northern Territory story, which Pat Anderson told twenty-one years ago at the National Press Club.

It's about an old man from the Top End. He's passed away now, but this is what happened to him. He was living quietly on an outstation near Kakadu. One day, some government workers drove up in a four-wheel drive while the old man was sitting out the front of his tin shed. He got up and introduced himself and showed them around a bit.

As they were leaving, they asked him if there was anything he needed.

"Oh yeah," he said, "if you're coming back out this way, you could bring me a couple of packets of tomato seeds. I'd like to try and grow a few tomatoes here for myself."

Well, the government workers went back to town and told their boss about the old man who wanted to grow tomatoes on his outstation. And their boss told her boss, and so on.

After a while, all these people start arriving at the old man's outstation. Geologists come and take soil and rock samples. Meteorologists arrive with all sorts of gadgets to measure wind speed and rainfall. Ecologists set up camp to study the ecosystem and do environmental impact studies. Agronomists arrive to do feasibility studies on market gardens in the tropics.

All the while, the old man sits in front of his tin shed, watching this very entertaining activity. Eventually, after several months, one of the scientists comes up to him and asks him how he is.

"I'm fine," says the old man, "but I'm still waiting for those packets of tomato seeds."

THE TORMENT OF OUR POWERLESSNESS

I begin with an observation by Yunupingu, following a meeting with Prime Minister Malcolm Fraser forty-six years ago:

> It is 1977. My father is still alive and I am on a boat with a new prime minister, Malcolm Fraser. He has defeated Gough Whitlam, who first met my family when he was a pilot in World War II. With me is Toby Gangale, the senior Gundjehmi leader, steering us to a place where barramundi swim. Fraser has asked us to fish with him, and we hope there are words we can say to him that will halt his changes to the land-rights laws and overturn the government's decision to mine at Ranger. But Fraser only thinks about the fish. The fish bite and Fraser starts to pull them in. "Look at this one!" he yells. I bait his line again. Toby is silent. "And again – a bigger one." He baits his own line now – getting the hang of it. "You beauty, a barramundi!" All the time I try and put words in his mind about the importance of land, about the importance of respect, about giving things back in a proper way, not a halfway thing. *But he has his mind on other things – he's not listening; he doesn't have to.* He just keeps catching barramundi, enjoying himself.

Yunupingu saw a succession of prime ministers visit his Country over the course of his life. When young, he helped draft the Yirrkala bark petitions, which were presented to parliament in 1963. They were a response to the federal government excising land from the Arnhem Land reserve for bauxite mining. The Yolgnu were not consulted. The petition states that the procedures of excision were never explained beforehand and were kept secret from them. It also states that when government officials "came to inform them of decisions taken without them and against them," the officials "did not undertake to convey to the Government in Canberra the views and feelings of the Yirrkala aboriginal people."

Sixty years since the Yirrkala petitions to the House of Representatives, Australia is going to a referendum for the first time in a quarter of a century, on a proposal aimed at mitigating the endemic, generational and structural problem of *not being heard*. As Yunupingu so eloquently recollected, *he has his mind on other things – he's not listening; he doesn't have to*. Parliaments do not listen because they do not have to. Governments do not listen because they do not have to. Bureaucrats do not listen because they do not have to. Aboriginal history is replete with examples of this.

In 1963, Aboriginal people were removed at gunpoint from their homes at Old Mapoon, in Far North Queensland. This followed the passage of the *Commonwealth Aluminiam Corporation Pty Limited Agreement Act 1957*, when 8000 square kilometres were excised from the mission reserve. Old Mapoon residents were removed by Queensland police in the dead of the night with *no notice*. No one was told. No one was consulted. The state government burned down the buildings and dwellings. The Cairns constitutional dialogue spoke of this as a history which Australians do not know. But the burning of 1963 is still remembered:

> Mapoon people have remained strong, we are still living at Mapoon. Mapoon still exists in western Cape York but a lot of our grandfathers have died at New Mapoon. That isn't where their spirits need to be.

In 2001, Premier Peter Beattie formally apologised to the people of Mapoon.

Another example is from 1998 and the Native Title negotiations following the High Court's *Wik* decision. The negotiations excluded Indigenous leaders. Mick Dodson wrote at the time:

> What I see now is the spectacle of two white men, John Howard and Brian Harradine, discussing our native title when we're not even in the room. How symbolically colonialist is that?

In 2007 came another devastating example of not listening: the Northern Territory Emergency Response, a major policy disruption in which the government chose to take an extreme decision and introduce a suite of draconian laws without talking to the communities it affected. That was despite the inquiry report that was the catalyst for the intervention – *Ampe Akelyernemane Meke Mekarle*, "Little Children Are Sacred" – leading off with this:

> In the first recommendation, we have specifically referred to the critical importance of governments committing to genuine consultation with Aboriginal people in designing initiatives for Aboriginal communities, whether these be in remote, regional or urban settings.

The inquiry, led by Patricia Anderson and Rex Wild, found that consultation needs to be carried out with great care, because a lot of "what is first said by Aboriginal people in remote areas is not, in fact, what they want, but either what they think the mainstream culture wants them to say or what they think the mainstream culture wants." This is an important finding because it explains why the routine consultation of the bureaucracy never elicits the buy-in or legitimacy required for government policies to work. Anderson and Wild stated that constructive consultation is an "ongoing process" that is built over time – not a one-off – and requires the state to seek out views that "represent all members of the community and not just those of one family or of the 'community manager.'" The report argued that good consultation leads to "ownership" by communities of the solutions and "strength" being returned to Aboriginal people. There is consensus in both Indigenous communities and the bureaucracy that the Emergency Response failed because the Commonwealth failed to consult.

In 2004, the abolition of the Aboriginal and Torres Strait Islander Commission (ATSIC) by Prime Minister John Howard was another decision taken without consulting Indigenous representatives. Despite a contemporaneous review of ATSIC that recommended the devolution of power to the regions, and amendments that would enhance the political participation of women, the Howard government sought to abolish it entirely, with the support of the ALP. Howard declared he would mainstream Indigenous services.

At the time, the Opposition spokesman, Senator Kim Carr, noted presciently that this would see "indigenous peoples' power in this country diminished, their capacity to engage in society diminished, their capacity to engage in the economy diminished." Undeterred, the prime minister and the Minister for Indigenous Affairs, Senator Amanda Vanstone, announced that in replacing ATSIC they would "appoint a group of distinguished indigenous peoples to advise the Government." According to Vanstone, a "tremendous amount of goodwill" was sufficient to improve the lives of Indigenous Australians.

Professor Kerry Arabena observed that the new arrangements would see the silencing of independent voices, and that:

> In future, it is likely that there will be an increasing distinction between "service delivery" and "advocacy" agencies and a void of any representative role for Indigenous peoples with which to engage with government and each other.

There are far too many examples of this void across the Federation to list, demonstrating the trajectory of powerlessness and voicelessness that has led to this year's referendum. Yunupingu succinctly summed up the problem: *they do not listen because they do not have to.*

Since the 1967 referendum, when it gained the power to make laws for Aboriginal people, the federal government has always required some kind of advocacy mechanism, a credible and authoritative group to consult on the laws and policies it wanted to enact: first, the National Aboriginal Consultative Committee, then the National Aboriginal Conference and the Aboriginal Development Commission. But the chopping and changing of such mechanisms has a destructive impact upon communities: their funding, short-term and long-term planning, quality of health, social cohesion and hopes for the future.

There is no requirement to consult before abolishing statutory, non-constitutional bodies and there is no requirement to replace them. This renders representative bodies subservient to the government of the day. A Voice cannot be truly independent or offer frank advice if it lives with the threat of abolition. It alters the efficacy of communication and dialogue if the existence of the mechanism is predicated on obsequiousness towards the state.

Another way that the state neutralises mechanisms of listening and hearing is through the bureaucracy. While all state and territory governments support a "Yes" result in the referendum, over the decades governments have become accustomed to "listening" to First Nations communities in a variety of ritualistic ways: hand-picked advisory mechanisms, Acknowledgements of Country and an endless parade of posters and water bottles and wristbands. These are supposed to indicate connection and deep engagement. But the power imbalance remains.

Participating in these activities is a form of "regulatory ritualism." The term comes from the American sociologist Robert Merton, who identified five different ways people adapt to a prevailing order: conformity, innovation, ritualism, retreatism and rebellion. Ritualism means "the acceptance of institutionalised means for securing regulatory goals while losing all focus on achieving the goals or outcomes themselves."

Ritualism is rife across Australia when it comes to Indigenous policy. Ritualism permits street-level bureaucrats and the many government stakeholders who gorge from the billion-dollar taxpayer trough to do the things that denote social consensus on Indigenous policy – for example, Reconciliation Action Plans and Acknowledgments of Country – while masking their inaction on the things needed to secure the agreed goals.

One example is the corporation that displays an expensive Aboriginal art collection, champions NAIDOC morning teas, receives taxpayer subsidies to fund Indigenous cadets and endorsed the Uluṟu Statement *before* it became a referendum commitment. Symbolic gestures matter *until shit gets real*. The threshold of commitment is structural change. Giving Aboriginal people any substantive power becomes the problem. Closing the Gap is another example of state ritualism. Think of the Abbott, Turnbull and Morrison governments engaging in the annual ritual of a parliamentary speech lamenting "no change" to the gap.

The following three case studies are examples of how this plays out in Indigenous Affairs. In the example of child protection, the case worker is always regarded as the authoritative speaker, even when they are fabricating allegations and misleading the court. The second case study is the Abbott government's Indigenous Advancement Strategy. Besides the abolition of ATSIC, this policy setting was central to the wave of sentiment in the dialogues calling for a Voice. The final example is the way recent Coalition governments have craftily walked back the obligations given to them by the Australian people in the 1967 referendum.

Child protection

In 2016, I was approached by the NSW government to conduct a review of Aboriginal children in out-of-home care – in other words, child removals. I had not long completed an independent review into Queensland's youth detention centres as co-commissioner alongside Kathryn McMillan QC. The NSW review was initiated by Minister Brad Hazzard, who had been persuaded of the need by the compelling advocacy of the Grandmothers Against Removals, or "GMAR," an alliance of Aboriginal grandmothers who had been advocating for the return of their grandchildren.

In preparation for this undertaking, I read everything I could about the child protection system and Indigenous children, and listened to the recording of the forum where GMAR secured the promise of a review from the minister. The stories they shared were woeful, exposing blundering and unskilled conduct by case workers. I recall thinking: how can it be that the dominant narrative positions Aboriginal parents as the problem? Stories were shared by the sector itself of poor practice, ineptitude and punitive case management by bureaucrats that most reasonable-minded Australians would be outraged by.

The review team conducted a deep dive into 1144 case files and found many mistakes and evidence of poor practice. We found removal documents prepared for court that did not match the case files. There were many failures by the department or the courts to scrutinise or check the veracity of case workers' claims. The court relies on sworn affidavits from case workers, which means the court is relying on hearsay rather than direct evidence. (This has been an issue in many other jurisdictions too.)

Grandmothers Against Removal submitted to the review that case workers regularly lied to the court. One common complaint was that case workers informed the Children's Court that they had attempted to prevent removal, but in reality "no real effort was made." Instead, the case files were replete with evidence of case workers failing to do the basic social work required to avert removal. If the court is not checking the work of the case worker because it presumes the Crown is a model litigant, and the department is not checking the case worker's statement to ensure it is factual and backed up with evidence of the assertions, there is no way to be assured that the basis for a decision on child removal is correct. This is a serious matter. It is a rule of law issue.

It was – and is – common for children to be removed from families because of the bureaucratic culture of risk aversion, lazy practice nurtured by poor oversight, and a system hiding behind an inviolable narrative that Aboriginal people are bad parents and architects of their own misfortune. My team were:

> perplexed to discover that FACS [the Department of Family and Community Services] provided the Children's Court with misleading or untrue evidence in a significant proportion of the case files that were reviewed. While it is possible that some of the mistakes and omissions could be attributed to human error, in some cases it was difficult to understand how the error could have occurred during the normal course of events. Broadly, the files reveal that on a number of occasions ... [case workers] overstated or exaggerated the factual evidence, minimised shortcomings in FACS casework, failed to identify relevant "strengths" of the parents, or concealed the "full picture" from the court.

To paint a clearer picture of what this looks like for the Aboriginal child, in one example a case worker informed the court that a child had "only recently" become aware of her Aboriginality, although the department had known for a long time. Such negligence has a colossal impact on a child's future. Flagging Aboriginality would open up the opportunity for the child to be cared for by family or kin under the Aboriginal Child Placement Principle. This would have an impact on the child's capacity to live on or near to Country, to live with or among their wider family network, which would routinely involve cousins and kin. This provides the vulnerable child with a support network.

In another example, the case worker told the court they had referred a child's parents to drug and alcohol counsellors, but no referral had occurred. This kind of lapse could hinder the restoration of a child to a family. One of the goals of case work after child removal is restoration. Often a plan is agreed upon so that parents have a tangible pathway to the return of their children. But a failure to have clear goals means there is no transparency to how a parent can have their child returned. Given the poor life outcomes for a child in out-of-home care, this is significant.

The lifetime impact of removal is incalculable. According to Professor Val Braithwaite and Mary Ivec, "Institutions of justice and welfare collide not only in child protection case work, but also in children's life trajectories." It is well established that child protection is a channel to youth detention. The result can be "cross-over children," Braithwaite and Ivec say, "whose early lives are defined by state care and whose later lives are defined by the criminal justice system."

In another case, the department informed the court that it was concerned about the "transience" of the children's mother and her children's exposure to domestic violence. Yet the mother had been in stable accommodation for three years, and the Department of Housing had provided evidence that she was not in a violent relationship. Again, these false statements can influence the decision to remove, as they did in these cases, and the consequences are lifelong for children.

The child protection system I reviewed, and overall, lacks transparency and appropriate oversight. There is no effective regulator. It is a closed system. There is no genuine consultation with the Aboriginal family or community. One of the flaws of the system is that the workforce has no professional accountability. Unlike for lawyers, doctors and teachers, there is no external regulator who is independent and can exercise authority over the profession. There are no formal consequences for poor practice. This lack of regulation influences case worker behaviour.

What was happening reminded many families of the autocratic state that subjugated Aboriginal people during the protection era. In the review, I found that some families fought hard, and others chose not to fight the system, concluding that they were powerless. It is a system that renders our people voiceless.

The lack of accountability means that Aboriginal people struggle to find an independent party to listen to their concerns. In the case of Grandmothers Against Removal, they relied on an informal regulator, the media, to prosecute their arguments. But informal regulators are not enough.

The department will from time to time make ad hoc changes in response to complaints. However, these tend to be cosmetic. This is regulatory ritualism. The rituals of listening to Aboriginal people include the way the bureaucracy enthusiastically embraced my review but didn't cooperate, or how departments appoint handpicked advisory committees for advice but never implement it, or how departmental walls are plastered with glossy brochures espousing case workers respect for "self-determination" when nothing could be further from the truth, or posters proclaiming the importance of the Aboriginal Child Placement Principle, when it's virtually never properly applied. None of this results in Aboriginal people's substantive complaints being listened to.

Three observations of this system justify the need for the Voice to Parliament. The first is that the review occurred because of Aboriginal activism. It should not be the case that street protest and media activism are the only ways Indigenous people can be heard. The Voice will be a mechanism to demand attention that sits *within* the structures of the state. It will allow the Indigenous community to flag issues that are important to them; they will have the ability to recommend that a representation is made about the issue by the Voice to the government or parliament. This means the ground-level impact of policies and laws upon families and individuals can be properly and seriously ventilated *in situ*, with the parliament. The gravity of such a representation, particularly on matters that are causing a huge amount of suffering and community disharmony and sadness, will guarantee a response.

The second issue is the ritualism that is common to most regulatory systems. The observations I made of the culture of the department in charge of child protection ring true more widely:

> Bureaucracy is a large beast that, we know from the research, takes on a life of its own, with its own practices, norms and culture. Often this culture can be indifferent or resistant to the intentions of legislators. This means that the regulatory framework – the laws and policies that govern a bureaucracy – often compete with, or are neutralised by, the dominant culture of a department.
>
> Mostly, employees have no choice but to adopt or conform to the culture of a workplace or department.

It is inevitable that street-level bureaucrats exhibit ritualism as a sign of deep-seated defiance of prescribed legislative goals. This can occur for many reasons. In my review, I found case workers who did not understand Aboriginal history or culture. Furthermore:

> As a caseworker, if the workplace culture is about risk aversion, as many are, then one is likely to minimise those innate skills that invite risk, such as intuition and instinct. Whatever the values of a department, caseworkers – as most employees will – conform.

This is complex and invites precisely the kind of scrutiny the Voice can bring to bear, as communities will ask their representatives, *Why is my son in out-of-home care? Why is my daughter in youth detention?* A Voice, because of its constitutional force, will be able to cut through bureaucratic culture, jargon and ritualism to identify the structural problems and find solutions to some of the nation's most intractable challenges born of poor administrative accountability.

It is important to make clear that most bureaucracies and bureaucrats would welcome this. The work of child protection, especially case work, is complex and stressful. The impression I formed during the review was that many case workers felt their work and the pressures they face are incomprehensible to anyone outside the system. The stress of making decisions that will affect a child for their entire life is compounded by the complexities of working in a huge bureaucracy. Of course, this is not dissimilar to the perspective of the Indigenous people they service, who equally feel their life experiences are not able to be understood by case workers.

The third connected observation is that the Voice's work can supersede departmental reviews, commissions of inquiry and Royal Commissions. Australian governments have a propensity to use these as mechanisms to listen to Indigenous peoples. But such inquiries are often used as a can-kicking exercise that allows a government to defer matters to the next term of parliament.

While child protection is a state responsibility, Senator Jacinta Price recently argued that it should be assumed by the Commonwealth. The example is a useful one, because the issue of children in Alice Springs is being deployed by the Dutton Opposition as a reason to reject a constitutional Voice. But child protection is an incredibly complex field of public policy. Added to the complexity is the outsourcing of protection work, often to a stressed and under-resourced Aboriginal sector. It is a space that is constantly changing and being reviewed. I found the sector difficult to navigate as a professor of law; I can scarcely imagine what it is like for Aboriginal and Torres Strait Islander families. My review found in interviewing them that many departmental case workers and bureaucrats did not understand the policies either. The knowledge deficit should not be so acute. This applies especially to the Aboriginal Placement Principle, which virtually no jurisdiction implements properly.

The complexity of the system is why it is so easy for the media to broadcast misinformation about child protection figures. The issue of crime in Alice Springs has been something that Peter Dutton and Jacinta Price have focused on in recent months as a reason not to have a Voice. In travelling to Alice Springs, they have a national press pack follow them, through which they are able to amplify their case for the status quo. When Peter Dutton read out Northern Territory notification statistics, I thought: there is so much complexity to unpack in that data. And my short explanation above of poor and misleading practice highlights that reading isolated data is not sufficient to understand what is going on. My review found that many children should never have been removed and many children should have been restored to their parents. The data Dutton highlighted is not a complete picture of what happens in child protection. Nor is the superficial explanation of the problem in Alice Springs adequate. A nuanced debate would involve discussion of the failure of the Northern Territory to spend the allocated budget it is given for Aboriginal people on Aboriginal people, of the failure of housing in the region, and the lack of access to the National Disability Insurance Scheme (NDIS) without such housing, of the children and young adults with undiagnosed fetal alcohol syndrome, and the failures of governance as a consequence of the abolition of ATSIC and the amalgamation of local councils, which led to the dismantling of local governance mechanisms. An enshrined Voice, one that is elected by communities, would have the status and power to paint a more fine-grained picture from the ground. History is often key to understanding regional situations. The paucity of knowledge about Aboriginal history in many instances feeds the failure to find solutions.

Indigenous Advancement Strategy

The most criticised policy raised universally by the constitutional dialogues was the Indigenous Advancement Strategy (IAS), introduced by Tony Abbott's government. Yet few Australians know anything about this primary driver of a Voice.

When the Abbott government was elected, Indigenous programs, grants and activities were moved to the Department of Prime Minister and Cabinet. In May 2014, the Indigenous Advancement Strategy was announced. This policy saw $534 million stripped from the Indigenous Affairs budget.

Communities said there was no consultation. The Australian National Audit Office confirmed that there was a "lack of consultation with Indigenous communities prior to the implementation of the Strategy." There was no review of programs and activities to determine what worked and what did not work. Overnight, communities were disrupted by this extraordinary piece of policy that took a razor to programs that had been run for decades, including men's groups and the award-winning women's night patrols that protect women and children from violence. (The audit office would later validate everything the community was saying in the dialogues about lack of consultation, no evaluation of efficacy of programs, sudden withdrawal of funding and arbitrary decision-making on future funding.)

It is vexing to hear the current Opposition talk about women's issues as a reason against an enshrined Voice when it sliced and diced so many programs without any regard for evaluation. Community leaders talk about the stress of working in an environment that makes such dramatic changes to policy without notice. The process for reapplying for funding was unwieldy. Applications had to be made online and for many communities the system was difficult to navigate.

Well-resourced not-for-profit organisations, NGOs and corporations were competing with communities for the same money. The former groups have the staffing levels and IT resources to allocate to this time-consuming activity. This was not the case for communities. The IAS was for most communities a disempowering and demoralising experience. The audit office found that "Small organisations lacked the resources to complete a competitive application, with the open tender process favouring large, non-Indigenous, non-governmental organisations." The IAS list for successful organisations for funding – competing against the Indigenous community – included the federal government departments of health and ageing, education and training, sport and recreation, justice and attorney-general, and correctional services. Sporting organisations, such as Swimming Australia, Athletics Australia, Rugby Australia, the Queensland Rugby Union and the Australian Football League, received Indigenous funds. Several universities received funds. Noel Pearson said at the time, "Most Australians have no idea that the greatest beneficiaries of investment of indigenous funds are non-indigenous organisations not based in the communities in whose name the expenditure has been justified by parliament."

Reporting on the IAS was difficult because service providers declined to comment on their funding for fear of losing future financial support from the government. This is what we also heard during the dialogues – fear of punitive government and bureaucracy. The media and the Indigenous Affairs department were not allowed in the room so that participants could be frank and tell the truth of their experience without fear of losing funding.

Under the IAS, communities reported lost funding or partial funding of youth programs. Wendy Morton, CEO of the Northern Territory Council of Social Service, said programs primarily working with young people had been hit, and "We've heard stories like this from Tennant Creek, Alice Springs and Darwin." The Central Australian Aboriginal Legal Service (CAALAS) youth justice advocacy program, which works with young offenders in Alice Springs, said it had not received enough money to fund a single staffer. The government's response was to parrot its empty catchphrases – "children to school," "adults into work," "safe communities" – without any evidence that its policy settings ever achieved these. The Closing the Gap record over this period suggests that it was never successful in getting children to school and adults into work or in ensuring communities were safe.

The allocation of funding to non-Indigenous organisations was particularly galling because the Aboriginal sector – the ecosystem misleadingly and erroneously termed the "Aboriginal industry" – had been devastated by the IAS. Many organisations shut down or were forced to let staff go. The audit office found that the funding decisions made by the department did not reflect need and lacked transparency. And given the current fearmongering regarding the Voice, it is worth noting that the office found the Coalition's "strategy did not reduce red tape."

In 2015, Patrick Dodson said that bureaucrats and top-down decision-making were responsible for waste in the sector: the mass job losses in

Aboriginal organisations were a "recipe" for welfare dependency. Fred Chaney said the IAS was "bogged down in bureaucracy":

> It is likely that the confusion, delays and uncertainties created by the implementation of the IAS destroyed significant value in Indigenous organisations, and in particular human capital, through delays imposed on functioning organisations, defunding of local organisations and resulting loss of employment.

Indeed, the story of the IAS and the discretion of the Minister of Indigenous Affairs to approve use of the funding continued. It was reported in 2018 that Minister Nigel Scullion, a member of the National Party, had used IAS funds to fund the Northern Territory Cattlemen's Association to argue a "detriment" case under the *Aboriginal Land Rights (Northern Territory) Act*. To argue a detriment case is to argue *against* the approval of an Aboriginal land claim. Scullion also provided $155,000 to the Amateur Fishermen's Association of the Northern Territory (AFANT), which has said its "aim is to ensure no detriment to recreational fishers as part of future native title grants." One news outlet reported that the association had confirmed the department approached it, and that the $155,000 was indeed partially used to fund legal fees, "because AFANT was a small operation" and "collecting evidence of detriment is easier with a lawyer." It was reported that the money used to hire lawyers to argue against Aboriginal land rights came from the culture and capability division that funds "Indigenous cultural expression and conservation" and "participation in the social and economic life of Australia."

In any event, the outrage of communities about the IAS fuelled support for the Voice. The affected communities and organisations saw constitutional recognition in a new light – as an opportunity to address their voicelessness and powerlessness. The backlash became so significant that Noel Pearson, Patrick Dodson, Kirstie Parker (co-chair of the National Congress of Australia's First Peoples) and I met with Prime Minister Tony Abbott to argue for a comprehensive consultation with Aboriginal and Torres Strait Islander peoples. Abbott resolved to meet with key leaders. Forty met with the prime minister and Opposition leader Bill Shorten at Kirribilli in July 2015. The weekend before, the Aboriginal and Torres Strait Islander leaders met to agree on the direction of constitutional recognition. A statement was drafted to convey to Prime Minister Abbott and Opposition Leader Shorten, which became known as the Kirribilli Statement. This was the moment when merely "symbolic" recognition was taken off the table by the to-be-recognised. I take up this narrative later in the essay.

Closing the Gap: Walking back 1967

One of the driving forces of the 1967 referendum was the abysmal job the states and territories were doing of managing Indigenous affairs, and the associated appalling treatment of Aboriginal and Torres Strait Islander peoples. Deplorable living standards, eroding protection infrastructure and the negligence and disregard as draconian laws gave way to integration and assimilation – all of this was visible to the Australian public. The referendum result allowed the federal government to take control and nurture a coherent approach across the nation to Indigenous welfare and advancement.

Since that time, Indigenous affairs has oscillated between the centralising tendencies of the Labor Party and the eschewing of federal responsibility by the Coalition. According to constitutional lawyer Dylan Lino, the main rollback began in the 1990s, with the Howard government's diminution of Indigenous rights to land and heritage, which "violated political conventions of Commonwealth beneficence established since the 1967 referendum."

In 1998, during the republic debate, ATSIC chairman Gatjil Djerrkura warned of the vulnerability of the 1967 commitment in the absence of further constitutional recognition: "We will be asking for constitutional recognition of our rights. Our experience with governments leaves us all too aware of the uncertain nature of their interest and commitment and the fragile nature of the spirit of 1967."

The most dramatic turn has been in the past decade under Coalition governments, in particular when it came to Closing the Gap. Closing the Gap is a complicated policy for any Australian, whether they be bureaucrat or citizen. It is never clear who is in charge, what the targets are and why the gap is not closing.

One of the most authoritative voices on Indigenous policy is a former head of the Indigenous Affairs portfolio, Michael Dillon. In the absence of media coverage, it was through his analysis that many Aboriginal people came to appreciate what happened to the first Closing the Gap arrangements and why they failed. Of the new arrangement, Dillon says the Australian government has "off-loaded significant policy and financial responsibility to the states and territories."

During the federal Coalition's recent time in office, most state and territory Labor governments felt that they had to step up on many Indigenous matters in the face of federal inertia and lack of leadership. While chair of the House of Representatives Standing Committee on Indigenous Affairs, Liberal MP Julian Leeser claimed that:

> Despite the popular conception, and the power given to it in 1967, the federal government is not responsible for much that happens in the lives of most Aboriginal Australians. These matters are still largely the province of the states and territories. Like almost every other area of policy, the Commonwealth is just the ATM.

But the Uluṟu dialogues did not see the Commonwealth as "just the ATM," not in theory or practice. No one in the constitutional dialogues ever spoke of the states and territories as being the primary partner in Indigenous affairs. In fact, the Morrison government's talk of "local voices" and "regional voices" was not how communities referred to themselves. They are an artefact of bureaucracy and the way the state views things. Borders are imposed; they are not how Aboriginal people see the continent.

Closing the Gap was launched in 2008 by the Rudd government. By 2018, it had not succeeded in meeting the bulk of its targets on health, life expectancy and economic opportunity. In September 2020, Dillon said that, going into the negotiations on a new agreement, the Commonwealth had an interest in shifting political and financial responsibility for Indigenous services to the states and territories "to the maximum extent possible," an objective that he calls the "fiscal federalism driver." Dillon argues that:

> The Commonwealth's success in avoiding responsibility is not just about Closing the Gap. It is the culmination of a decade-long push to shift Indigenous policy responsibilities away from the Commonwealth and towards the states and territories, and away from Indigenous-specific programs and towards mainstream programs. On issues as diverse as heritage protection, essential services, Indigenous housing and legal aid, the Commonwealth has been reducing its footprint. Where it retains responsibility – in relation to income support, for example – it has increasingly turned to mainstream programs rather than Indigenous-specific ones. The new Closing the Gap agreement is a major capstone on a pre-existing trend that will shape Indigenous policy for generations.

In a later research paper, Dillon argues that instead of adopting a national perspective, the Commonwealth is adopting the role of just another jurisdiction. It is taking minimal responsibility for the quality of the state and territory responses. The government is setting up a position where it can criticise the states for any failure to close the gap in the future, rather than seeing itself as responsible for the overall national outcome.

Dillon also notes that funding for the refreshed agreement does not match the original funding, and that the Australian government "has no intention of matching the investment levels of the first decade of Closing the Gap."

For its part, the Close the Gap Campaign Steering Committee's ten-year review found that the twenty-five-year program was "effectively abandoned after five years" because the "architecture" to support it (namely, national approach, national leadership and funding agreements) had "unravelled."

The National Indigenous Reform Agreement report was even more direct: "implementation fell away as National Partnerships expired and were not renewed," "federal–state cooperation on resourcing significantly diminished mid-way through the 10-year timeframe and ... with few exceptions, expired funding agreements were not replaced," "leveraging of mainstream funding was not fully realised and fell away with time," and "the key oversight and implementation bodies were disbanded from 2013–14."

This is an extraordinary story of prime ministers delivering the annual Closing the Gap statement, reporting on progress or no progress, espousing aspirations to close the gap but making decisions to dismantle key arrangements, including leadership and funding. Not once did a prime minister admit publicly that this was the government's actual policy.

Later in his paper, Dillon writes that:

> This strategy has been pursued incrementally, without explanation or announcement, hidden in plain sight. It has been obscured by the sheer technical complexity of the issues involved, and by an incessant focus on meeting the Closing the Gap targets to the exclusion of the necessary complementary focus on ... the appropriate design and focus of substantive policy reforms.

This speaks to the way the Voice will have the capacity to seek information on changes and not sit back and wait to be consulted or rely solely on the information the government gives it.

This analysis applies to the first iteration of Closing the Gap. The second iteration – led by the Coalition of Peaks, a group of eighty Indigenous community control representatives and some of the nation's most experienced Indigenous bureaucrats – was predicated on thorough Indigenous-led consultation and refocused attention on access to data. It is too early to judge its success. Regardless, the Albanese government has the unenviable task of walking into a policy setting which the conservatives negotiated that does not appear to be working and is hard for the broader Australian community to follow. Despite how difficult it is for ordinary, non-expert minds to understand the complexity of Closing the Gap agreements, this has become the sole barometer of progress in Indigenous affairs and policy, or so the public has come to see it.

Who is entitled to speak?

Too often, politicians and pundits have done exactly as predicted by the men and women at the Rock six years ago: they have reduced the matters raised at Uluṟu to an ideological football game. The inferior quality of the debate should not come as a surprise. From 2012, it was apparent to me that politicians and their advisers did not read the reports produced and did not have accurate information about the public processes in train.

I have heard from many Australians that this is the case across the board with politicians and their staffers because of their enormous workload. Having said that, in the field of Indigenous affairs it does mean politicians are not reading the solutions set out by successive reviews and inquiries, but rather are unilaterally coming up with proposals based on anecdote or the last person who had access to them. Scrutiny of this – who has access to Parliament House and who is wandering the floors lobbying – is essential to understanding whether these inside players truly represent the communities they purport to represent.

On constitutional recognition, at each meeting, for each prime minister, each new Indigenous Affairs minister, we had to explain the process from scratch. Tom Calma, a former Aboriginal and Torres Strait Islander Social Justice Commissioner, used to say to us as younger Aboriginal leaders, "leaders are readers." You cannot lead if you do not read. Yet the National Party rejected the Voice in 2022 and committed to a "No" vote before even knowing the substance. I was outraged that a professional political party could do such a thing: reject a major reform without reading the detail. Particularly a party that had held office for the past decade and managed the Indigenous Affairs portfolio for most of that time. Any reasonable mind would query their ability to assess the efficacy of Voice design, given their record. Dear reader: *it's not good*.

Yunupingu observed of politicians that when you raise Indigenous issues with them, "their minds are always somewhere else." It is a look in their eyes when they are calculating that your issue has no bearing on the next election. That you and your interests fall outside of the issues facing most

Australians. This is the reality of majoritarian ballot-box democracies. This is why constitutional reform is vital for the future of Indigenous Australia. The utilitarian ethic of liberal democracies means that Aboriginal peoples' political and legal concerns are dwarfed. Three per cent of the Australian population take on the epic task of convincing Australian parliaments and the executive of the utility of passing laws or adopting policies that appear to benefit Aboriginal people alone, but in fact benefit all Australians.

One of the most pernicious aspects of having no authoritative Voice is the way credibility is afforded to politicians above actual community members. Consider Opposition leader Peter Dutton's deployment of the word "academics." He often repeats the charge that the Voice will be composed of sixteen "academics." Alternatively, there are his persistent references to "the Canberra Voice" and the "elites," a sweeping sociological term that can mean many things.

The National Party, in its dismissal of the referendum, was exercising a social power that First Nations people do not have. The point is not made to the Nationals leader: "Mr Littleproud, the Uluṟu dialogues were also driven by a desire for less bureaucracy." Rather the question is constantly put to Aboriginal people: can you assure us the Voice will not lead to more bureaucracy?

Yet the National Party does not know why the Voice is needed. Nor is it asked to account for its position; instead, it is free to make sweeping generalisations about bureaucracy, black elites and Indigenous academics. The Liberal Party does not know why the Voice is needed. But its reasons for "No" are not scrutinised in the same way as the arguments for "Yes" are, even though its governance failures are one of the primary justifications for the Voice. (Never mind that its own policies in government created *more* bureaucracy.) Indeed, it is the "No" case that feels free to question the credibility and identity of those who speak for the Uluṟu case. And too often the media then reinforces the power imbalance with its reporting.

The philosopher Miranda Fricker has written on this economy of credibility, which she calls "epistemic injustice." Epistemic injustice raises questions about who knows what and who speaks for whom and it is an issue to grapple with for the referendum. The question "How will the Voice work?" is a legitimate one, but it is muddied by social power and, consequently, the credibility that the speaker can garner to speak with authority. Often those without power suffer from what Fricker calls "a credibility deficit."

The Australian Reconciliation Barometer measures how many Australians have met an Indigenous person, and the numbers are low. The need for the Voice is best articulated by Aboriginal people who have experienced voicelessness (an experience shared by most First Nations people). This explains why the "Yes" vote hovers around 51 per cent for non-Indigenous people compared to 82 per cent for Indigenous people. Experience matters. And in its absence, credible voices are what is required to share knowledge and experience.

Decades ago, anthropologists were the most credible speakers on Indigenous affairs in Australia. They remain so in native title courts. On other matters of Indigenous policy, speakers such as Father Frank Brennan have been afforded greater credibility than Aboriginal community leaders. As Noel Pearson said to the Joint Select Committee on the Aboriginal and Torres Strait Islander Voice Referendum, in response to Brennan, "Frank supports the Voice but only on his terms. He only wants what Frank wants." The point Pearson was making is that too often policy is dictated by people who are disconnected from what the community needs, but who think they know best.

Fricker writes that "even the most hateful prejudicial ideologies may be sustained not only by explicitly hateful thought and talk but also by more domestic stereotypical ideas that are almost cosy in comparison." The "No" campaign is relying on these "cosy" stereotypes, which often go unquestioned by the hearer. This is what Dutton is doing when he uses the terms "elites" and "academics" and the "Canberra Voice." The philosophy of hearing and listening is dense and discursive. But this problem would be obviated if our voices could be heard.

Constitutional recognition belongs to that overarching category the "unfinished business" of the nation, a phrase used by Patrick Dodson, the grandfather of reconciliation, in his speech "Beyond the Mourning Gate." Unfinished business has at its core the "original grievance": the failure to recognise the ancient Aboriginal polities that coexisted on this continent for well over sixty thousand years. Their societies and laws were disrupted by the British arrivals. The land was taken without recognition or compensation. It is this fact that is the source of grievance to this day.

Australia is unique in its foundation story, as the British Crown provided no legal recognition to the Aboriginal people of the continent as collectives or polities or of their land rights. The messiness of the reception of British law, and the irresolution of the relationship between the Crown and the multiple Aboriginal sovereignties of the Australian continent, has led to ambiguity when it comes to the telling of Australian history and the legal status of Aboriginal peoples. The failure to recognise Aboriginal people has meant that the legitimacy of Indigenous peoples within the framework of the Australian state has been continually questioned and undermined. Andrew Fitzmaurice, in his book *Sovereignty, Property and Empire 1500–2000*, writes of the dramatic consequences of non-recognition for indigenous peoples:

> Those societies that were swallowed up by the settler societies also had their claims to property and sovereignty almost entirely buried by the doctrine of terra nullius.

At the Uluṟu convention, one of the motivations for writing "Our Story"– the history that sits in the broader recognition document we call the Uluṟu Statement from the Heart – was to set out the mosaic of Aboriginal and Torres Strait Islander laws that existed before the arrivals. First Nations explain their Law to Australians in this way:

> **OUR STORY**
>
> Our First Nations are extraordinarily diverse cultures, living in an

astounding array of environments, multi lingual across many hundreds of languages and dialects. The continent was occupied by our people and the footprints of our ancestors traversed the entire landscape. Our songlines covered vast distances, uniting peoples in shared stories and religion. The entire land and seascape is named, and the cultural memory of our old people is written there.

This rich diversity of our origins was eventually ruptured by colonisation. Violent dispossession and the struggle to survive a relentless inhumanity has marked our common history. The First Nations Regional Dialogues on constitutional reform bore witness to our shared stories.

All stories start with our Law.

THE LAW

We have coexisted as First Nations on this land for at least 60,000 years. Our sovereignty pre-existed the Australian state and has survived it.

We have never, ever ceded our sovereignty.

The unfinished business of Australia's nationhood includes recognising the ancient jurisdictions of First Nations law.

> "The connection between language, the culture, the land and the enduring nature of Aboriginal law is fundamental to any consideration of constitutional recognition." (Ross River)

Every First Nation has its own word for The Law. Tjukurrpa is the Anangu word for The Law. The Meriam people of Mer refer to Malo's Law. With substantive constitutional change and structural reform, we believe this surviving and underlying First Nation sovereignty can more effectively and powerfully shine through as a fuller expression of Australia's nationhood.

The Law was violated by the coming of the British to Australia.

This truth needs to be told.

As legal scholar Paul McHugh discussed in *Aboriginal Societies and the Common*

Law, aside from military force it was the British law that most shaped the colonial encounter:

> It provided a key intellectual means by which the arriviste dealt with the fact of aboriginal presence. Sometimes that response involved a wilful blindness, as in the terra nullius fiction developed in Australia to explain its constitutional foundation ... [But] once the aboriginal peoples had been truly subdued physically, white lawfare assumed a new, more meddlesome role inside tribal life ... [It was the] heart of the intellectual armoury of white domination, particularly in the suppressive "twilight century" after the massive dispossessions of the late nineteenth century.

According to McHugh, "Like it or not, [Aboriginal groups and individuals] had no option but to participate inside the common law constitutionalism that had engulfed them." Or, to put it another way, from the time of the British arrival, the descendants of this continent's most ancient polities have been active participants in the democratic governance of the colonial states and then the federated nation. I say active because we have always challenged the political system, asserting our rights and reminding the state of the unresolved original grievance. We were advocating for roles in the democratic life of the state long before we were advocating for a treaty.

This is demonstrated in the early calls for recognition in parliament. In 1927, Fred Maynard wrote to the NSW premier asking for the control of Indigenous affairs to be transferred to an Indigenous board. Joe Anderson, taking the name King Burraga, chief of the Thurawal tribe, argued for self-determination and Indigenous representation in federal parliament in 1933. In 1937, Yorta Yorta leader William Cooper requested representation, as did Pastor Doug Nicholls in 1949. In 1988, the Barunga Statement called for a national elected Aboriginal and Islander organisation to oversee Aboriginal and Islander affairs.

At the same time, we have, as peoples, with no interruption, asserted our sovereignty since 1788. This is neither a radical claim nor mere exhortation.

It is a fact. It is always going to be a relevant factor in constitutional recognition. In 2011, the expert panel sought advice from barrister Bret Walker SC to clarify the law pertaining to Aboriginal claims to sovereignty:

> The basis of settlement of Australia is and always has been, ultimately, the exertion of force by and on behalf of the British arrivals. They did not ask permission to settle. No-one consented, no-one ceded. Sovereignty was not passed from the aboriginal peoples to the settlers by any actions of legal significance voluntarily taken by or on behalf of the former or any of them.

Some Aboriginal people fret that constitutional recognition could cede their sovereignty. But there has always been, to some extent, constitutional recognition of our people and none of it has had any impact upon claims to Aboriginal sovereignty, including at Federation, in 1967 and today: in their treaty discussions, both the Victorian and Queensland governments acknowledge that Aboriginal people never ceded their sovereignty. (Even though state sovereignty is not a word invented by Indigenous people – it is a Western concept of absolute power and authority, usually secured through conquest of territory and possession of property.)

The lack of formal recognition by the British Crown from first contact did not render Aboriginal people entirely invisible. We, as Aboriginal peoples, were recognised in the instructions sent by the British Admiralty with James Cook to "observe the genius, temper, disposition and number of the natives, if there be any, and endeavour by all proper means to cultivate a friendship and alliance with them."

We were recognised in the instructions to take possession of the country, which stated this should be done with our consent:

> You are also with the consent of the natives to take possession of convenient situations in the country in the name of the King of Great Britain, or, if you find the country uninhabited take possession for His Majesty by setting up proper marks and inscriptions as first discoverers and possessors.

We were recognised by Arthur Phillip when he was commissioned to sail a first fleet to Australia to establish a settlement, as his instructions urged him "to endeavour by every possible means to open an Intercourse with the Natives and to conciliate their affections, enjoining all Our Subjects to live in amity and kindness with them."

We were recognised in the declarations of martial law by colonial governors and recognised in English parliamentary committees as news "trickled" back to London of the "unequal conflict." We were recognised in the newspapers that kept count of our dead and in the editorials which debated our status in our own country: was the indiscriminate killing of Aboriginal people murder if they were British subjects; or, on the other hand, if they were not British subjects, were extrajudicial and unconstitutional measures justified in a war with Aboriginal nations?

We were most certainly recognised in the constitution by virtue of our express exclusion: a type of non-recognition. And as our numbers dwindled because of the frontier wars, indiscriminate killings and exposure to European diseases, we were recognised as vulnerable and "doomed" in the many "protection" acts legislated by states and territories that curbed our freedoms and subjugated us.

Yet throughout this we have survived. We have advocated strongly for a voice, for a place in the Australian state. We have argued for fairness and equality. We have always known that the wellbeing and the future prosperity of the nation depends on our having equal rights. This advocacy has been almost Sisyphean. Why? Because "race" is allied to the nation's institutions and rules. It would take more than deleting the word "race" from the Australian constitution to remove such a salient feature of Australian democracy.

Australia was at the forefront of democratic progress and "colonial liberalism," yet while we celebrate world-famous achievements such as the secret ballot, this uniquely colonial Australian liberalism can be contrasted with the illiberal unfreedom with which Australia very deliberately treated the first peoples. Queensland historian Thom Blake describes this in his book *A Dumping Ground: A history of the Cherbourg settlement*, the settlement my own great-grandmother was removed to from Warra:

> In the early months of 1901, as white Australians were undergoing their rite of passage into nationhood, another group of Australians were also participating in a rite of passage – but of a quite different kind. In the Burnett district of south-east Queensland, remnants of the Wakka Wakka tribe were being rounded up and dumped on a reserve on the banks of Barambah Creek. From camps on the fringes of towns and station properties, they had been forced onto an Aboriginal settlement established ostensibly for their care and protection. For the Wakka Wakka, their "rite of passage" was not into nationhood or independence but into institutionalisation and domination. The two rituals were diametrically opposed.

It cannot be said that Australian democracy was a smooth translation of the racial superiority of the "Old World" British establishment to the "New World," because, as historian Marilyn Lake describes, the Australian colonists strived to distinguish themselves from the Old World. In part, this was driven by "memories of class rule" and rejection of the elitism of the English polity and the pursuit of a more egalitarian society.

> In the self-governing Australasian colonies of the late nineteenth and early twentieth centuries, governments elected by manhood (and increasingly womanhood) suffrage inaugurated a series of radical democratic experiments – including the Australian ballot, the eight-hour day, the abolition of plural voting, public ownership of utilities, a legal minimum wage, wages boards and arbitration courts, workers' compensation, the abolition of child labor, immigration restriction, the political enfranchisement of women, the first children's court, mothers' pensions and a maternity allowance, old age and invalid pensions – inaugurating a reform regime described by contemporaries as "state socialism." Progressivism was defined by a shift away from a reliance on charity and philanthropy

> to remedy social ills toward a vision of the state as a vehicle for achieving social justice.

There is much in this vision that endures today, some of which forms a shared commitment across the political spectrum. Ann Curthoys and Jessie Mitchell note that this narrative emphasises, as well as rejection of Old World class constraints, the peaceful nature of Australia's political evolution:

> Historians often tell it, to Australian audiences at least, as part of the positive story of colonists emerging from the shame and restrictions of penal settlements to build a free society with liberal institutions such as freedom of the press, trial by jury, freedom of assembly, and, with self-government, the development of democratic institutions such as universal male suffrage and the secret ballot. Part of the attraction of this narrative of progress is the rapidity of change with little in the way of violent struggle, and the making of democratic institutions from such an unlikely start.

It is the case, however, that Australian progressivism also "justified the possession of new lands" and animated "intense land hunger."

> The democratic passion for equality expressed a repudiation of Old World hierarchies and privilege but led in turn to new oppressions, evident in the exclusion of indentured and "coolie" labor and "Asiatics" more generally, the expulsion of Pacific Islanders, the segregation of African Americans, and the destruction of indigenous communities, whose "inevitable disappearance" shaped dominant narratives of settler nations.

As Lake observes, "progressive reforms could have profoundly undemocratic outcomes" and this included the exclusion of Aboriginal people from the voting franchise.

We were pioneers and innovators, of a peculiarly Australian form of governance: democracy *and* race. Curthoys and Mitchell say, "the supposed mundanity of the tale of the rise of Australian democracy and independence is arguably the key to its subtle appeal; this is a reassuring history of progress without fuss, of a people who established governance over a continent without bloodshed or serious division."

Indeed, the most mundane feature of the colony was the conflict and the bloodshed, not the democratic innovations. Noel Pearson says of this:

> From the oral histories of Aborigines and from the documented sources of colonial times – referring to the death of Aborigines on the frontier speak to me of the profoundest moral problem of this history: the heavy discounting of the humanity of the Aborigines. It is not the horrific scenes of mass murder that are most appalling here; it is the mundanity and casual parsimony of it all.

The voluminous literature that exists on this issue, including colonial parliamentary reports and modern parliamentary reports, makes it difficult to reconcile the routine nature of the killings with the lament "Why weren't we told?" To say this is not to diminish the enormous impact of Henry Reynolds' book of that name. There is, however, a convenience to this "truth" – in the same way that there is a convenience to the attribution of early Australian attitudes to the fixed inheritances of Empire. The evidence is persuasive that the innovations of Australian democracy were allied to the innovations of race policy. And this has reverberated down the decades for Indigenous Australians in Australian democracy.

What does repair look like?

The question then arises: how do democracies move on from frontier massacres and forced racial segregation and the many manifestations of protection legislation, such as stolen children and stolen wages? Many societies pursue recognition as a way of accommodating indigenous peoples within the framework of the state. The strong end of the spectrum involves the recognition of rights that empower indigenous peoples or else prohibit the state from doing something such as passing racially discriminatory laws.

Constitutional lawyers like to distinguish between big "C" constitutional recognition and little "c" constitutional recognition. Big "C" recognition may involve an alteration to the text of the Australian constitution and little "c" reform is change to the constitutional system more broadly, its public institutions, laws and conventions. Over the years in Australia, this has involved statutory land rights recognition, cultural heritage, native title recognition and recognition of Indigenous polities through representative bodies.

The United Nations has studied the various arrangements that have been concluded between indigenous peoples and states over the years. Its study, the most comprehensive yet undertaken, found that consensual legal instruments and practical mechanisms to ensure better relations in the future fall into the following categories: "treaties," "agreements" and "constructive arrangements."

Both the Voice to Parliament and treaty fall within the UN definitions of treaties, agreements and constructive arrangements. Indeed, the UN special rapporteur on treaties cautioned against adopting a narrow definition of "a treaty" and "treaty-making," as it would hinder or pre-empt any innovative thinking in the field over the years.

This is where the Uluṟu Statement comes into the frame. The United Nations states that "it is precisely innovative thinking that is needed to solve the predicament in which many indigenous peoples find themselves at present." The Uluṟu Statement from the Heart is an innovative proposal.

Some say having a Voice to Parliament before a treaty is counterintuitive or goes against the grain of Aboriginal activism. Yet the sequence of the Uluṟu reform – Voice, Treaty and Truth – is consistent with Australia's legal and political culture. It is an Australian solution to an Australian problem.

Treaties were agreements signed mostly by the British Crown in North America and New Zealand. As the Special Rapporteur states: "Britain actually was the only colonial Power which conducted a consistent treaty policy with extra-European peoples. This tradition was continued by the Powers which succeeded Britain in the territories concerned."

There is generally no "best practice" when it comes to treaties, as most emerge from a distinctive history. First-contact treaties in parts of Canada and the United States were negotiated when the indigenous parties had leverage for foreign policy reasons and because Britain and France were competing for indigenous land and territory. These first-contact treaties are regarded as having an international character involving sovereign indigenous nations. This type of treaty will not be replicated in Australia. As academics Stephen Young and Harry Hobbs have argued, "The processes of colonialism and state formation [have] meant that agreements negotiated today are not international covenants between independent sovereign states."

The Uluru dialogues were particularly astute when they discussed and debated treaty. One challenging issue raised was the fracturing of social cohesion among nations, clans and families because of the native title process. This has exhausted or torn apart many families, and the fighting over Indigenous Land Use Agreements (ILUAs) meant many were sceptical of the capacity to negotiate fair treaties with the Crown when the power imbalance is so acute. The level of comprehension and experience of agreement-making was advanced. Many suggested dispute resolution services were needed before people could move on to treaty with the state. Victoria provided a very good example of why a Voice is needed first: who does the Commonwealth treaty with? In the absence of a Voice structure, it's difficult to understand how the Commonwealth can determine this.

Reconciliation

Besides granting rights, modern states also pursue reconciliation as a way of "reconciling" the relationship between indigenous peoples and the invader/colonisor. Reconciliation is the concept that many societies draw upon to repair harm. The twin pillars of reconciliation are regarded as truth and justice. "Truth" is about history, a better official account of what happened, and "justice" is the change required for "repair" to occur. A primary aim of reconciliation is to restore faith and trust in the state and its institutions. History and truth-telling play an important role in the restoration of trust in public institutions. Public education plays an important part alongside this, so that the public has a shared understanding of what happened, why it happened and how it might be prevented from occurring again. There is not one single approach to this: it may involve reparations, apology, truth-telling, criminal prosecution, public memorialisation and so on.

The reconciliation process in Australia was set up in the late 1980s and guided by the Council for Aboriginal Reconciliation. In origin, it was a contrivance manufactured by Bob Hawke and his Labor government, who could not deliver on a promise made by the prime minister for a treaty. According to Stuart Rintoul's biography of activist Lowitja O'Donoghue:

> On 5 June, as the promise of a treaty turns to a process of reconciliation, the legislation for a Council for Aboriginal Reconciliation is passed unanimously through the federal parliament. In a show of bipartisanship, Robert Tickner and his Liberal counterpart, Michael Wooldridge, shake hands across the parliamentary despatch box. But even the name of the council is a compromise. Tickner had intended that it would be called the Council for Aboriginal Reconciliation and Justice. Hawke's advisers felt that "Justice" went too far.

This framework was the first iteration of "can-kicking" by the Commonwealth – to avoid delivering "justice," which is more electorally controversial than a never-ending truth process that produces recommendations never implemented.

The council's work culminated in a major conference at the Sydney Opera House in 2000, when it released the Australian Declaration Towards Reconciliation and the Roadmap for Reconciliation. One of the key recommendations was that the state should pursue two things: structural reform – as in constitutional reform – and immediately tackling Aboriginal disadvantage. Not long after this, Howard rejected the decade-long reconciliation project and reconfigured the agenda to suit his own conservative ideas about Aboriginal peoples' place in the nation.

Howard divided reconciliation into the practical and the symbolic. This was a false binary, yet it endures to this day. The practical and the symbolic are two sides of the one coin. The practical aspect of reconciliation that Howard would champion was to do with citizenship rights: the universal right to education and employment. This fitted with Howard's policy of mainstreaming and dismantling Indigenous-specific services. The symbolic measures he eschewed were non-symbolic matters, such as land rights, Indigenous rights, constitutional recognition, treaty and anything substantive that would result in the redistribution of power. James Cockayne, the current NSW Anti-slavery Commissioner, observed then of the Howard approach:

> They seek to achieve reconciliation by providing "practical" measures such as improved service provision. This "Reconciliation" approach denies the utility of … treating indigenes as a distinct group with specific rights distinct from other Australians; to accept such distinct rights, to accept this difference, is perceived as tantamount to accepting the division of Australian "unity." Practical Reconciliation becomes a way of denying indigenous difference and its social and legal consequences.

Following the end of the Council for Aboriginal Reconciliation, a new entity was created: Reconciliation Australia. As Aboriginal rights went into abeyance, Reconciliation Australia sided with Howard. And from the Howard approach, the Reconciliation Action Plan (RAP) was born. Scholars who have studied Australia's reconciliation process from the outside regard it as the most unusual in the world. This is because it focuses on private action or corporate civic action, and not on truth and justice. According to the American sociologist Charlotte Lloyd, who has studied Australia's RAP system, ours is the only process that asks nothing of the state.

Lloyd describes this approach as "creative reconciliation," as it provides practical actions for citizen engagement and corporate citizenship, so that reconciliation is not left entirely to the government. Lloyd's conclusion, though, is that Reconciliation Action Plans do not "invite the deep consideration of violent and racist policies of the Australian state that led to current inequalities." Nor do they associate reconciliation "with structural political change such as land rights, indigenous sovereignty, or treaty." Even more importantly, she argues that:

> ultimately RAPs promote understandings of indigenous difference that leave organizations and their members ill equipped to understand persistent sources of conflict in indigenous and non-indigenous relations, particularly those stemming from indigenous aspirations for social change.

These same concerns for the shortcomings of reconciliation were expressed in the constitutional dialogues that led to the Uluṟu Statement from the Heart.

The Australian experience demonstrates a thin commitment to reconciliation by the state. This is because while truth and justice are the twin pillars of reconciliation, the justice component is often detached from truth. The justice component is important because it can lead to recommendations for change and reform. Truth-telling cannot have the desired effect if it is detached from the structural and systemic reforms that are needed for change. To that end, the truth-telling aspects of the *Bringing Them Home* report and other inquiries and reviews have been effective when they have painted a picture for Australians of structural injustice.

Charlotte Lloyd studied thirty-four Reconciliation Action Plan vision statements; none expressly mentioned racism as an obstacle to reconciliation. Only two mentioned fairness and justice. Acknowledgements of Country and Welcomes to Country do not change the law. They do not change the legal frameworks that disempower communities. Moreover, the RAP program does not "encourage organizations to think of themselves as political actors," but rather "positions Indigenous difference as an object for private voluntary action rather than public political obligation."

Having said that, Reconciliation Action Plan participants understood and embraced the Voice to Parliament proposal immediately. This is because many of them have a "voice to" – a norm of consultation with their Indigenous workforce, as in the Australian Rugby League's Indigenous Council. The emphasis on "having a say" in practical matters helped the sector's comprehension of the Voice. This was an unexpected consequence of Australia's unconventional approach to reconciliation.

It was the Uluṟu Statement from the Heart that recalibrated the skewed reconciliation process in Australia and brought truth and justice back to the table. It had been twenty years in the wilderness. The correction began with the expert panel appointed by Julia Gillard. I served on that panel. I was in my early thirties.

The terms of reference required the expert panel, among other things, to report to the government on "possible options for constitutional change to give effect to Indigenous constitutional recognition." The panel developed a formula to assess each constitutional option. For the panel to recommend a proposal, it had to: contribute to a more unified and reconciled nation; be of benefit to and accord with the wishes of Aboriginal and Torres Strait Islander peoples; be capable of being supported by an overwhelming majority of Australians across the political and social spectrums; and be technically and legally sound. This formula was adopted by later processes, but in time became utterly subjective, especially the criteria of technically and legally sound.

The expert panel recommendations included that section 51(xxvi) of the constitution be repealed. Section 51(xxvi) is called the race power. This section was amended in the 1967 referendum to remove the words "other than the Aboriginal people in any State." This removal conferred upon the federal parliament the power to make laws with respect to Aboriginal and Torres Strait Islander peoples. The power authorises beneficial laws and adverse discrimination. The deletion of section 51(xxvi) and the insertion of a new power to make laws for Aboriginal and Torres Strait Islander peoples, called section 51(a), was the new proposal. Another feature of section 51(a) was adding introductory words to the new head of power: a statement of recognition.

The placement of the recognition statement within a head of power was because of the legal complexity of preambles. There cannot be a preamble to the UK act and you cannot simply place a preamble at the beginning of the Australian constitution because of interpretive challenges. There was also a view that a preamble at the beginning of the constitution, especially if it contained a no legal effect clause, was tokenistic.

The proposed introductory words of section 51(a) were:

- Recognising that the continent and its islands, now known as Australia, were first occupied by Aboriginal and Torres Strait Islander people.
- Acknowledging the continuing relationship of Aboriginal and Torres Strait Islander peoples with their traditional lands and waters.
- Respecting the continuing cultures, languages and heritage of Aboriginal and Torres Strait Islander peoples.
- Acknowledging the need to secure the advancement of Aboriginal and Torres Strait Islander peoples.

The fourth recital to section 51(a) was meant to provide some guidance to the parliament in its work and to the High Court in its interpretation of the intent of the section: to secure the "advancement" of Aboriginal and Torres Strait Islander peoples. This was controversial because no one could guarantee the High Court would interpret "advancement" in a way that Indigenous people would view as beneficial. There is a subjectivity to that word. And if that could not be guaranteed, then the change is the same as the status quo.

Another recommendation was for a new section 116(a). Section 116(a) was a non-racial discrimination clause. It was a recommendation that the expert panel drew from the constitutional concern after *Kartinyeri* (the 1998 Hindmarsh Island Bridge case) that the race power could be used to pass laws that single out Aboriginal people for adverse discriminatory treatment. *Kartinyeri* involved the Howard government's use of the race power to stop Ngarrindjeri Aboriginal women invoking the *Aboriginal and Torres Strait Islander Heritage Protection Act* 1984 to prevent a bridge being built over a cultural place of significance for women. Howard passed the *Hindmarsh Island Bridge Act* 1997 so that the *Aboriginal and Torres Strait Islander Heritage Protection Act* had application everywhere in Australia except for the Hindmarsh Island Bridge area.

The Ngarrindjeri challenged the decision, arguing that the race power as amended in 1967 could not be used adversely against Aboriginal people. The High Court found there was no limitation on the power. The judgement is not definitive in the sense that it incontrovertibly supports adverse legislation, but it definitely leaves open that possibility.

Even so, section 116(a) was regarded as tempering the power of the Commonwealth to pass discriminatory laws, such as those in *Kartinyeri*. Australia's commitment to the principle of racial non-discrimination is accepted in all Australian jurisdictions. The *Racial Discrimination Act* binds the states and territories, but not the Commonwealth parliament, which can disallow provisions of the act to permit discriminatory laws. The Commonwealth parliament would have an additional burden placed on it.

Despite the work of the expert panel, there was a distinct lack of appetite for the reform of section 116(a): non-response from the ALP and outright rejection by the Coalition of a non-discrimination clause. From 2011 to 2015, the expert panel recommendations were whittled down to a modest form of recognition promoted by the Recognise campaign. This campaign had been set up by Labor to ensure that the next Coalition government would not kick the can down the road on a referendum, and it was funded by Reconciliation Australia. The task for Recognise was community education, but it was actively involved in the politics of the referendum. In the absence of any definitive reform idea, Recognise projected a vague but symbolic version of recognition.

As noted earlier, in 2015, Noel Pearson, Patrick Dodson, Kirstie Parker and I met with Prime Minister Tony Abbott and Opposition Leader Bill Shorten to make the point that the apparent crystallising of bipartisan support for a referendum on a symbolic form of recognition, supported by the Recognise campaign, would not be something that would be supported by most First Nations communities. We said a new process would be required before we could move to a referendum.

Abbott listened to what we had to say, did not necessarily agree, but committed to a meeting. Before the meeting, forty Aboriginal and Torres Strait

Islander leaders gathered over the weekend at the Museum of Sydney to caucus. Afterwards, the leaders released the Kirribilli Statement to make it clear that constitutional recognition, as a symbolic statement of recognition or mere acknowledgement, would not be acceptable. We stated:

> Any reform must involve substantive changes to the Australian Constitution. It must lay the foundation for the fair treatment of Aboriginal and Torres Strait Islander peoples into the future.
>
> A minimalist approach, that provides preambular recognition, removes section 25 and moderates the race power [section 51(xxvi)], does not go far enough and would not be acceptable to Aboriginal and Torres Strait Islander peoples.

The Kirribilli leaders recommended that there be a dialogue between Aboriginal and Torres Strait Islander peoples and the government to negotiate the proposal to be put to a referendum. The Kirribilli Statement also called upon the government and the Opposition to identify what they would support in the way of constitutional recognition.

By this time, in 2015, "recognition" was a dirty word, not only because of the Recognise campaign but mainly due to the Coalition government's Indigenous Advancement Strategy and the WA remote community policy, which threatened to "close" between 100 and 150 Indigenous communities. The words "recognise" and "recognition" excited either hostility or ambivalence, because the dictionary meaning is acknowledgement, conveying, in a legal sense, a reform that is symbolic yet non-substantive. Yet no one had agreed to that minimal vision of recognition.

Of course, the preference of the political elite at this time was for something like an "acknowledgement" or "a statement of fact," without any legal effect. But this would never and will never receive the majority support of Aboriginal and Torres Strait Islander peoples. While symbols are important to Aboriginal culture, the constitution is not for symbolism. It is where the real business of the nation is set down. It is where the powers of the Commonwealth and the states are defined and distributed.

It was around this time that I became interested in the political theory on polities that are never listened to and feel unheard. I know it is not fashionable to say such things, but I am not a lawyer who has ever been fully interested in theory. I am sure it is a major flaw, but I was more interested in the practical application of the law, where the law gave rise to problems and how to fix those problems.

But the thing I could not shake from my head was watching the prime minister and Opposition leader sit at the head of the table while forty people from forty communities spoke about the structural problems their communities faced. What is it like to be the leader of a nation and encounter a polity that is profoundly unhappy?

At this time, as one of the main Indigenous lawyers working on constitutional reform, I found it difficult to understand why politicians failed to hear what First Nations leaders and community members were saying. I had a textbook idea about how political and law reform work, but none of it applied to our people.

There were two challenges I saw. One is that politicians meet with Aboriginal leaders on a myriad of issues, but often First Nations do not feel heard and politicians and advisers do not listen.

The second is the impact of telling your story over and over again and not being heard – what effect does this have on health and wellbeing?

I found solace in theology and the work of the Old Testament scholar Walter Brueggemann, particularly his writing on the subversiveness of hope:

> Hope, on one hand, is an absurdity too embarrassing to speak about, for it flies in the face of all those claims we have been told are facts. Hope is the refusal to accept the reading of reality which is the majority opinion; and one does that only at great political and existential risk.
>
> On the other hand, hope is subversive, for it limits the grandiose pretension of the present, daring to announce that the present to which we have all made commitments is now called into question.

Brueggemann's writing is profound; for me, it spoke to the experience of communities believing that change would come even if those in power did not. The continual refrain of government was not to be ambitious; politicians would glibly cite the referendum record as incontrovertible evidence that the nation cannot change. Or we were lectured about political pragmatism, even though the proposed reform was itself a pragmatic one. Or we would encounter the old chestnut – which politicians, advisers and lobbyists don't appear to realise is patronising and the subject of much civilian ridicule – that the perfect is the enemy of the good and politics is the art of possible. Meh.

I vividly remember reading Hans Vaihinger's *Die Philosophie des Als Ob* or *The Philosophy of "As If."* Vaihinger's argument was that most of our thoughts are fictions, because often in life we can only proceed "if what we know to be false is true" because it serves a purpose to think that way. We must have multiple ways of understanding and thinking about the world. As Kwame Appiah put it, "it is a gentle jeremiad against theoretical monism."

I wondered, too, about the connection between wellbeing and the sense of being heard. I had heard spurious and over-egged claims that symbolic recognition can improve health, but the evidence for this is weak. Yet it seemed to me that poorer health outcomes manifest when the world abandons you and you fail to have your voice heard. Serendipitously, a US scholar, Jill Stauffer, published a book that same year, 2015, on the consequences of the failure to hear. Stauffer writes about a concept of "ethical loneliness," which is the "experience of having been abandoned by humanity compounded by the experience of not being heard."

> It is the isolation one feels when one, as a violated person or as one member of a persecuted group, has been abandoned by humanity, or by those who have power over one's life's possibilities. It is a condition undergone by persons who have been unjustly treated and dehumanized by human beings and political structures, who emerge from that injustice only to find that the surrounding world will not listen to or cannot properly hear their testimony – their claims about what they suffered and about what is now owed them – on their own terms.

Stauffer writes about the decision humans make to disengage, so as to protect themselves from the continual let-downs and put-downs from, and disappointment with, those whose job it is to protect them. It seemed to me that this experience had occurred too often for our people. When we travel to communities, even to this day, Aboriginal people talk about how this experience makes us "sick."

Stauffer talks about the issue of repair and the importance of asking what repair looks like after injustice. Stauffer says that "ethical loneliness" is:

> caused not only by dehumanization, oppression, and abandonment but also by the failure of just-minded people to hear well – from those who have suffered – what recovery or reconciliation after massive violence or long-standing injustice would require.
>
> Such failures of hearing haunt sites where the goal is political transition, reconciliation, or forgiveness. As such, unassuaged ethical loneliness has political ramifications.

This goes to the heart of the reconciliation project in Australia: the failure of just-minded people to hear well – from those who have suffered – what recovery or reconciliation after massive violence or longstanding injustice would require.

The reconciliation process and its crown jewel, the Reconciliation Action Plan, did not involve repair. And in 2014 and 2015, as politicians and the Recognise campaign kept talking about symbolic recognition, I wondered why it was they could not hear what our people were saying "repair" is; and that it is not symbolism alone.

This is the core of reconciliation:

1. Recognise the harm that was done; and then ask
2. What does repair look like?

Recognition is part of what repair looks like.

After Abbott was ousted, Malcolm Turnbull set up a new process, led by what he called the Referendum Council. Its members, of which I was one, decided to undertake deliberative dialogues on recognition. We met in late 2015 and early 2016 to sketch what these dialogues would look like. We discussed the opportunity for constitutional recognition. We knew that the government would not give us substantial resources to conduct dialogues and so we needed to ensure that our methodology would produce a robust sample of the Indigenous community.

We reflected on who we are as multiple polities. We have a deep connection to the land. We are a collective and we are a gerontocracy. Therefore, we decided that to have cultural authority, meaning within our culture, our elders would be dominant participants in the dialogues. This is why so many land councils were selected to run the dialogues.

We also believed it was important to ensure that the organisations on the ground that care for our communities had an allocated number of positions. Finally, we wanted to ensure that the many different men and women and young people in community who might be interested in participating in a constitutional process would have an allocation. It became apparent that the money required to run thirty-two to thirty-five regional dialogues was not going to be available. Therefore, we were forced to cut the dialogues to twelve dialogues in twelve regions. Statistically the dialogues were a robust sample.

We did not want the process to be a tick-and-flick process, which is what we were hearing about the way the Commonwealth and the states, territories and local governments consult communities on the ground. Like FIFO workers, bureaucrats would fly in and fly out of Aboriginal communities in a day.

We wanted these communities to grapple with national constitutional recognition and what "recognition" meant in their own region, as well as to respond to the many options that Shorten and Turnbull had agreed for us to put on the table. The prime minister and Opposition leader received our letter that set out the options we would take out for consideration, including treaty and a Voice to Parliament. By now the Voice had crystallised as one of the leading reform options. Both leaders agreed to this open-ended approach. In recent months, many Coalition politicians have reverted to saying that constitutional recognition is symbolism, but the reality is that by 2016, as letters were exchanged and permission was given to the process, it was evident that recognition could not be conflated with symbolism.

Meanwhile, I had been researching many constitutional processes around the world, studying deliberative democracy mechanisms, such as those used in Ireland, to think of the most appropriate ways to engage people in complex law reform. Professor Cheryl Saunders recommended to me the work of the Centenary of Federation committee and its work in Australian schools and communities. Their method involved scaffolding with civics education and it was tried and tested.

In a different way, I was attracted to the writing of the theoretical physicist David Bohm on "dialogue." He speaks of a capacity for creativity rather than the standard tick-and-flick consultation or poorly run events with ill-prepared facilitators that I had often experienced over the years in Aboriginal Affairs. Bohm talks about the Greek word *dialogue*; *dia* meaning "through" and *logos* meaning "word." It evokes the image of a stream of meaning "flowing among and through us and between us." Bohm says, "It's something new, which may not have been in the starting point at all. It's something creative. And this shared meaning is the 'glue' or 'cement' that holds people and societies together." Bohm goes on to say:

> Contrast this with the word "discussion," which has the same root as "percussion" and "concussion." It really means to break things up. It emphasizes the idea of analysis, where there may be many points of view, and where everybody is presenting a different one – analyzing and breaking up. That obviously has its value, but it is limited, and it will not get us very far beyond our various points of view. Discussion is almost like a ping-pong game, where people are batting the ideas back and forth and the object of the game is to win or to get points for yourself.

> In a dialogue, however, nobody is trying to win.
>
> Everybody wins if anybody wins.
>
> There is a different sort of spirit to it.
>
> In a dialogue, there is no attempt to gain points, or to make your particular view prevail. Rather, whenever any mistake is discovered on the part of anybody, everybody gains. It's a situation called win-win, whereas the other game is win-lose – if I win, you lose. But a dialogue is something more of a common participation, in which we are not playing a game against each other, but with each other. In a dialogue, everybody wins.

In many ways, this is the antithesis of adversarial party politics.

A subcommittee that included Noel Pearson, Pat Anderson, Dalassa Yorkston and me worked to pull together an agenda for a dialogue lasting three days. The first year, 2016, saw us travel the continent, testing the methodology and the process. We received substantial feedback and criticism and refined the final program.

Day One involved explaining the process and the history of advocacy and what the word "recognition" means, including for a particular region. It was important for the dialogue to be about regional nuances. Day Two involved a civics lecture about Australia's legal and political system and a legal lecture on the options for reform agreed to by the prime minister and Opposition leader, as well as a series of breakout groups and plenary sessions. A first series of breakout groups was based on the options. Following a report back to the whole gathering, we would then run a second breakout session but cross-pollinating the groups so that each had one person who was knowledgeable about each legal option.

Day Three involved reflections and agreement on the record of meeting. This was pulled together by the Indigenous working group leaders, who would meet to draw out the key quotes and ideas. The record sought to capture the spirit of the dialogue and the length and breadth of people's views, from radical or extreme to more conservative. Everyone needed to agree before the record of meeting could be finalised. This is how the habit of consensus was formed across the process.

Twelve dialogues were run from 2016 to 2017 and a National Constitutional Convention was then held at Uluru in May 2017. This was not a pan-Aboriginal process but one that was deeply rooted in the local; and while the reform was a national one, it is a mistake to say it was top-down, given the process.

The Referendum Council report states:

> The Dialogue process was unprecedented in our nation's history and is the first time a constitutional convention has been convened with and for First Peoples.
>
> This is the most proportionately significant consultation process that has ever been undertaken with First Peoples. Indeed, it engaged a greater proportion of the relevant population than the constitutional convention debates of the 1800s, from which First Peoples were excluded.
>
> The process led to consensus at Uluru.

There was something true in what Bohm had theorised about common participation, "in which we are not playing a game against each other, but with each other." The dialogues spoke to the creativity of our people, and to the power of cooperation. This bodes well for the constitutional Voice.

Voice, Treaty, Truth

Every regional dialogue ranked the Voice first as a priority in their region. When discussing the Voice alongside the racial non-discrimination option (section 116(a)), it was felt that the Voice would become a "front end" political limit on the parliament's powers to pass laws that affect Aboriginal and Torres Strait Islander peoples. By contrast, the section 116(a) option would be more of a shield than a sword. Rather than having to utilise the section 116(a) provision when faced with discriminatory legislation, and having to raise funds for litigation, which is prohibitive for most communities, and anticipate the thinking of High Court justices and then wait for a High Court judgement, a Voice would enable communities to be involved in the democratic decision-making of the state. In this way, it was hoped, a Voice would result in better-designed policies from the outset.

Much has been made of the sequence of Voice, Treaty, Truth. After diligent consideration in all the dialogues, the Voice was sequenced ahead of treaty. Treaties were underway at a state level, with South Australia predating Uluru and Victoria contemporaneous with it. But the offer on the table was constitutional recognition. As I asked in the 2021 Mabo Oration:

> What sense did it make, and does it still make, to defer or set aside the constitutional recognition and commence on treaty, especially when the federal Coalition has not committed to a treaty?
>
> Treaties that are not premised on the country's federal structure are not binding treaties. The Commonwealth constitutional power to override the states will always exist. The Commonwealth overrode the Northern Territory on euthanasia laws and has recently cancelled Belt and Road agreements entered into by the Victorian government with Chinese entities. Furthermore, political change at the provincial level also makes state-based treaties vulnerable. South Australia is a good example of what can happen with a change from a Labor government to a Coalition one. No treaty process is guaranteed. Victoria, the Northern Territory and Queensland are yet to be tested by a change in government.
>
> Perhaps the most salient issue concerning state-based treaties is their quality. Will they amount to anything more than service-delivery agreements? Without the fiscal dominance and capacity of the Commonwealth government, what financial resources do these state and territory governments have to underwrite their treaty commitments? These provincial agreements may be strong on the rhetoric, but without the over-arching legislative power of the Commonwealth Parliament and its financial capacity, they will be nothing like the treaties envisaged by advocates since the 1970s.

Truth-telling is third in the sequence. The dialogues spoke of Aboriginal and Torres Strait Islander history as being fundamental to recognition in a relational sense:

> "Cook did not discover us, because we saw him. We were telling each other with smoke, yet in his diary, he said 'discovered.'" (Torres Strait)

In the regions, quiet contemplation was given to the question: do our fellow Australians want to know more about our experience in our own country? The Ross River dialogue put it this way:

> Participants expressed disgust about a statue of John McDouall Stuart being erected in Alice Springs following the 150th anniversary of his successful attempt to reach the top end. This expedition led to the opening up of the "South Australian frontier" which led to massacres as the telegraph line was established and white settlers moved into the region. People feel sad whenever they see the statue; its presence and the fact that Stuart is holding a gun is disrespectful to the Aboriginal community who are descendants of the families slaughtered during the massacres throughout central Australia.

The dialogue schedule was altered on the first day to accommodate this lament about history and its connection to today's law. There was a universal view that the public record of Australian history, for want of a better description, failed to include their stories.

The Uluṟu delegates spoke of local history that is rarely promoted to a national audience. They spoke of truth-telling led by Aboriginal and Torres Strait Islander peoples working in their local towns and regions and cities, now alongside non-Aboriginal people. This work is being undertaken with councils, local history societies, libraries, schools and community groups. Historian Penelope Edmonds has explained that locality is key because so many individuals and communities are wary of attempts at reconciliation led by the government.

For example, there are the families of frontier officials who want healing and connection with the descendants of those who were killed. There is the Butchulla Warriors Monument in Queens Park, Maryborough, Queensland, the WA Carrolup Elders Reference Group and the Collection of Carrolup Children's Artwork in Perth, the Ration Shed in Cherbourg where the community has reclaimed the old girls' and boys' dormitories, and the Myall Creek Massacre Commemorations. And of course, there is the exemplary work of the YooRook Commission in Victoria, Australia's first truth commission, which has very effectively used its inquiry function to extract admissions from Victoria Police about its conduct on child removals. It seems this commission of inquiry model is better equipped for contemporary scrutiny of state conduct than for historical truth-telling.

I have been quite critical of a sole focus on off-the-shelf overseas truth commission models. After twelve years as a United Nations expert in this field, I can say that it is not done particularly well. Scratch the surface and the story of how victims or Indigenous peoples feel after such processes tells of mixed outcomes. We know the acute failures of the South African Truth and Reconciliation Commission. We also know that four such processes in Canada have had very little impact on Canadians' understanding of the truth of their history and their relationship with indigenous peoples.

Having a truth and reconciliation commission will not signal that truth-telling has occurred. In fact, we have experience in these truth-telling processes already, most famously with the Royal Commission into Aboriginal Deaths in Custody and the National Inquiry into the Separation of Aboriginal and Torres Strait Islander Children from Their Families. Australia adores a commission of inquiry or a royal commission to manage issues that governments of the day do not want to address. The truth-telling I have described at a local level is what empowers our people. However, we must be vigilant that, in giving freely of emotions and time, our people are not made sick through the telling of stories producing more reports and recommendations that collect dust on the shelves, and that the settler preference for healing is not about avoiding the pursuit of justice.

The *Voice in the Constitution*

There are those who have sought to forestall the constitutional voice by arguing that a legislative voice is a better first step. However, one of the stories we heard repeatedly was that with every political cycle, every three years, our representatives and service providers must troop off to Canberra to curry favour with the newest government and the newest minister. The experience is exhausting and demoralising. The durability and certainty of the Voice will be critical to its effectiveness. As the Referendum Council summarised, "The logic of a constitutionally enshrined Voice – rather than a legislative body alone – is that it provides reassurance and recognition that this new norm of participation and consultation would be different to the practices of the past." Constitutional enshrinement refers here to the establishment of the Voice in the text of the constitution. This does not mean the entire framework of the Voice model would be included in the text of the constitution. Rather, what would be incorporated into the constitution would be a reference to its primary function of providing advice to the parliament.

The deferral of detail to parliament is a normal approach to constitutional amendment. This is because principle is for the constitution and detail is for the parliament. Constitutions do not contain over-elaborated provisions. They do not contain bricks and mortar. They contain principle, in this case the principle that the government and the parliament should consult First Nations peoples on laws and policies made about their lives. Detail is left to the parliament. This is the bread-and-butter role of parliamentary representatives, to work on detail. The Australian people voting "Yes" at a referendum opens the door to the principle. On the other side is a design process with First Nations communities that is then submitted to a parliamentary committee for all Australians to contribute to. The *Aboriginal and Torres Strait Islander Commission Act* was one of the longest legislative debates in the history of Australia. There is no doubt that the Voice legislation will be the same.

This approach is how the High Court of Australia, for example, is recognised in the Australian constitution. The court came into force in 1901, but the detail was passed in legislation several years later. Matters such as Voice membership and location and selection procedures will be determined by a consultation process and negotiated through the parliament. Voting on a full-blown legislative model risks the Voice as voted on in 2023 being regarded as the Voice that Australians endorsed. While the legal risk here may be less than the political risk, the two-stage approach enables the Voice to operate flexibly and allows parliament to change it over time.

There is an argument from some that constitutional enshrinement of an institution is no guarantee that it will be set up or that it will continue to exist. The example used is an institution recognised in section 101 of the constitution called the Inter-State Commission, which no longer exists. I would argue this is an ahistorical example and that it was abolished for many reasons. The enshrinement of the Voice is a different case. The referendum in 2023 will provide legitimacy to it as an institution. While constitutional entrenchment does not guarantee existence, it is greater protection than legislation alone.

A legislated-only Voice is the status quo. It will be subject to the whims of politicians who hubristically believe they know better and can speak on behalf of Aboriginal people. The history of representative bodies since the 1970s shows that a legislated Voice can be abolished. Constitutional enshrinement will ensure that the Voice can frankly and fearlessly speak truth to power, something that legislated representative bodies cannot do. Pat Anderson warned in her *Little Children Are Sacred* report that in tick-and-flick, "like it or not" consultations Aboriginal people won't tell you the truth, they will tell you what you want them to say. I remember watching the Nationals Minister for Indigenous Affairs Nigel Scullion on Sky TV not long after the Uluṟu national convention. He told the Sky commentator that he travelled widely around the Northern Territory and no Aboriginal person had ever raised the Uluṟu Statement with him. Besides asking myself the question, "Is he really oblivious to the acute power imbalance?", I thought how a benefit of the Voice would be that ministers can no longer get away with such untested anecdote. The Voice will give a face and a name to the men and women of our communities who engage with the executive. No longer will First Nations people have to kowtow and suffer the indignity of unaccountable executive power.

I think here of some words from the report of the Royal Commission into Aboriginal Deaths in Custody, in 1991:

> Government can transform the picture of Aboriginal affairs. But not so much by "doing" things – more by letting go of the controls; letting Aboriginal people make the decisions which government now pretends they do make. Government would be doing non-Aboriginal society a service; the resolution of the "Aboriginal problem" has been beyond the capacity of non-Aboriginal policy makers and bureaucrats. It is about time they left the stage to those who collectively know the problems at national and local levels; they know the solutions because they live with the problems.

Section 129 – the words to say it

The constitutional provision we negotiated with the government reads:

> Chapter IX Recognition of Aboriginal and Torres Strait Islander Peoples
> 129 Aboriginal and Torres Strait Islander Voice
>
> In recognition of Aboriginal and Torres Strait Islander peoples as the First Peoples of Australia:
>
> i. There shall be a body, to be called the Aboriginal and Torres Strait Islander Voice;
> ii. The Aboriginal and Torres Strait Islander Voice may make representations to the Parliament and the Executive Government of the Commonwealth on matters relating to Aboriginal and Torres Strait Islander peoples;
> iii. The Parliament shall, subject to this Constitution, have power to make laws with respect to matters relating to the Aboriginal and Torres Strait Islander Voice, including its composition, functions, powers and procedures.

The Voice is in a new chapter of the constitution. It is a new section, 129. It is written to be consistent with the other clauses of the constitution. It exemplifies the distinction between principle and detail by containing the skeletal framework of the body in the constitution, with the design features left to the parliament.

Clauses (i) and (ii) of the new section 129 entrench the features of the Voice. Clause (i) states that there will be a "body" called the Aboriginal and Torres Strait Islander Voice. It uses "Aboriginal and Torres Strait Islander" as the name of the body. This is a term familiar to the Australian legal system. There is no legal implication in the chosen name. The constitutional position and functions of the Voice will be controlled by the substantive constitutional provisions and not by the chosen name. Two terms were contemplated: "First Nations" or "Aboriginal and Torres Strait Islander" Voice. However, during the dialogues across the continent, "First Nations" was not universally accepted. It was regarded as a North American term, relatively recent in its adoption and use, and not all land councils and their traditional owners supported it.

Parliament has the express power to make laws with respect to the Voice. This power recognises the Voice as sitting within the body politic and not outside of it. This flows from the Uluṟu Statement itself, which states that the "ancient sovereignty" of First Nations as a "spiritual notion" can with constitutional recognition "shine through as a fuller expression of Australia's nationhood."

Clause (ii) of section 129 has been drafted to create a body of Indigenous peoples able to provide advice to parliament and government through "representations." This word was carefully chosen to be respectful of Australia's federal arrangements and to establish that the Voice will speak on behalf of the Aboriginal and Torres Strait Islander community. The Voice is guaranteed the capacity to make representations to parliament and the executive government "of the Commonwealth." It has a broad scope so that it can make representations on specific issues relating to Indigenous peoples.

Clause (iii) establishes that the parliament will have the primary role in determining the composition, functions, powers and procedures of the Voice. Its power is not limited to those matters but is general in also extending to making laws "with respect to matters relating to the Aboriginal and Torres Strait Islander Voice." This power is expressed in the broadest possible terms and could cover things such as the legal effect of representations by the Voice and the ability of the Voice to speak to other bodies.

Two matters have caused media controversy about the constitutional provision: the reference to the executive and justiciability. They are related matters. I say media controversy, because the weight of legal opinion is not in favour of the concerns raised by self-described "constitutional conservatives." The executive power is included in the provision because the most unaccountable group in the system with the most power over the day-to-day lives of First Nations peoples is the bureaucracy. The Referendum Working Group was unanimous in its advice to Prime Minister Albanese that the executive be included. It was always envisaged that it would be. It was also discussed in the Uluṟu dialogues. Only those with little knowledge of Indigenous affairs could object to the inclusion of the executive.

Its inclusion raised questions about justiciability – the potential for judicial review – but these are minuscule and exaggerated. The final report of the referendum parliamentary committee reveals this concern is not acute. As Bret Walker SC said in his testimony to that committee (and incidentally, he has the largest constitutional practice before the High Court in Australia):

> It just seems to me that this notion that there is an implication threatened in the proposed subsection two, whereby the validity of executive action – multifarious decisions, great, small and middling, by officials great, small and middling – will be somehow jamming the courts from here to kingdom come as a result of this enactment is really too silly for words.

Walker condemned the suggestion that the court will be inundated by a "mythical procession of meritless cases":

> I don't think there's any prospect if this is put into our Constitution that a ten-year review ... will reveal that litigators have been run ragged keeping up with a deluge of cases. It's nonsense.

Cumulatively, each clause operates to empower a new political institution called the Voice with an entrenched power to advise the federal parliament and executive. The Voice has no legal power beyond the ability to make representations, so its effectiveness and influence is contingent on the effectiveness of the Voice in fulfilling its mandate to represent the views of communities. It will need to be judicious in the representations it does make to have an impact on lawmaking and policy. The quality of representatives, whether elected or selected by community, is essential to its success. At the end of the day, the success of the Voice will rise and fall on the men and women who represent the voices of the community. Legitimacy of institutions derives from two things: design and decision-making about scope. There is a process that is planned for communities across Australia to have input into what the Voice looks like. The government has no pre-planned model except for a wealth of input from the regional dialogues, the Leeser/Dodson parliamentary committee and the Wyatt/Morrison co-design process. The likelihood of legitimacy is higher if many hands have input into the design. Then legitimacy will also be derived from the effective functioning of the Voice: by remaining sharply focused and driven by community interests and not spreading itself so thin as to be ineffective.

When the COVID-19 pandemic forced the nation into lockdown, Scott Morrison looked to the public health sector to shepherd us to safety, he looked to the economists for advice on the economy, and when he looked to the Indigenous realm, it was already locked down. Remote and regional communities were among the first to be alert to the emerging risk from Wuhan. The Aboriginal community-control sector and land councils worked together to shut gatherings down, so that they were safe from the coronavirus. This speaks to the capacity of our communities to look after their own: the right to self-determination.

It was a time of anxiety and panic and grief. It was also a period in which Australians experienced *unfreedom*. The loss of autonomy and the control exerted by state and territory and federal governments was experienced by all Australians. For older Aboriginal people, these types of draconian governmental controls on freedom of movement were not dissimilar to what they had experienced during the protection era.

The COVID experience was not shared equally across the nation. Segments of the community were treated differently. I recall someone on the North Shore tweeting a photo of a harbourside beach and saying that this was Sydney in lockdown. Meanwhile, in Western Sydney, police helicopters were a nightly intrusion and restrictions were enforced far more stringently than in more affluent parts of the city.

One thing that was interesting to me during this time was the proliferation of Acknowledgements of Country. I work at a university but in addition to my day job, through my constitutional law work with the Uluṟu Statement, I speak to many different sectors, from corporate to mining to banking to sporting organisations to religious groups to schools and the University of the Third Age. It was fascinating to witness the ubiquity of Acknowledgements on Zoom, Skype, Teams, Meet and Webex.

What was going on in the Australian psyche? It seemed to me that COVID was challenging to many Australians' sense of identity. We could not leave the country, many could not put feet on Country, many could not leave our homes. Who are we as Australians if we are not taking off and landing? People felt vulnerable and unsure of the future. But one thing they found solace in was Aboriginal culture. They felt connected to Country. People seemed to know the Country they were locked down on. It wasn't just a "left" political thing. The one thing that connected people to where they were in a time in crisis was the First Nation footprint they were locked down on. Australia Post even introduced a section on envelopes and parcels for Australians to write the name of the First Nation to which their item was directed. Aboriginal culture was what many Australians clung to: the spiritual, the feeling of being on Country. We have all felt that feeling of reassurance, gratitude and relief on the way home to Australian soil, but we still haven't dealt with the original grievance in the country on which we land.

Uncle Stan Grant Snr once said of language, it's not who you are, but where we are. Uluṟu is not about identity politics. It is about location. We are located on this land together. We coexist. The Voice to Parliament is not just about the parliament and the executive. The parliament and the executive are representatives of the *people*. It is a Voice to the People. It is a dialogue for time immemorial between the First Nations and the Australian people.

We live in an era of rapid and incontrovertible climate change. Our old people want peace for their country. This is a moment of transformation. It is a time for renewal. People are sick of the tired, feral, aggressive arguments of the past. They want progress on integrity, climate and Indigenous lives.

The Uluṟu Statement is an invitation, a gift to the Australian people. When people say this is about changing Australian identity, it's not. It's about location; we are located here together, we are born here, we arrive here, we die here and we must coexist in a peaceful way. We're about to face a serious existential crisis as a people, as humankind, as the climate changes and the planet warms up. The fundamental message that many elders planted in the Uluṟu Statement is that to face this battle together, the country needs peace, and the country cannot be at peace until we meet; the Uluṟu Statement is the beginning of that.

There is something called a "constitutional moment." It means that the possibility of change only comes around once in a blue moon. I used to raise this idea with the mob in the dialogues, particularly in response to the cynical and exhausted who profess that change cannot happen in this country. A constitutional moment suggests that we cannot predict how or why or when the stars align for major change. Although research does show that the unifying feature is not bipartisanship but a courageous leader.

Forty-seven years after the Yirrkala petition and months before the referendum, the old man passed away and will not live to hear whether the Australian people accept the invitation offered to them by the First Peoples of the continent. In his essay "Rom Watangu," Yunupingu put it like this:

> What Aboriginal people ask is that the modern world now makes the sacrifices necessary to give us a real future. To relax its grip on us. To let us breathe, to let us be free of the determined control exerted on us to make us like you.
>
> And you should take that a step further and recognise us for who we are, and not who you want us to be. Let us be who we are – Aboriginal people in a modern world – and be proud of us. Acknowledge that we have survived the worst that the past had thrown at us, and we are here with our songs, our ceremonies, our land, our language and our people – our full identity.
>
> What a gift this is that we can give you, if you choose to accept us in a meaningful way.

Here we are on the cusp of the first referendum in twenty years. While the "Yes" campaign speaks to an optimistic and inclusive future, with a practical change aimed at recognising and empowering First Nations, the "No" campaign is cynical, regurgitating tired slogans from the 1999 Republic referendum: "Don't Know, Vote No" and "Canberra elites." It deploys Howard-era concepts of unity, formal equality and bucketloads of misinformation and dog-whistling while manufacturing the convenient no-change theory that respectable and fair-minded people can indeed "Vote No." The

"No" campaign is pessimistic and frightened, reliant on much misinformation and hyperbole by a small cabal of Australian Tucker Carlsons – Australian democracy will be "destroyed," they declare, we'll all be rooned. Time will soon tell whether First Nations are the most *unloved*, in this referendum, which is about being the most *unheard*.

We have had hope, always. So many people, during those five years from Uluṟu to Albanese, had no faith in the Australian people or the capacity of the constitutional order for change. Six years later, we are here. As we slog it out on the road to the referendum, the Uluṟu dialogues will continue the approach we have adopted since Malcolm Turnbull's hasty rejection of the Voice: turn every "No" into a "Yes."

In the dialogues we said to people who felt cynical about the process that we must believe the world can change. Reform is only ever about imagination. We Aboriginal people must suspend our belief that the system cannot change. We must suspend our belief that the nation cannot change. Despite all that has happened to our people, we must dream of a better day. Since Uluṟu, as we have faced setbacks from time to time, I have often recalled the words of Hans Vaihinger: "Sometimes, in thinking about the world, the truth isn't what you need."

NOTES

3 "invitation", "walk with us" and other excerpts throughout the essay: Referendum Council, *Uluru Statement from the Heart*, 2017.

4 "While it is not true": Niki Savva, "Next to Albanese, Dutton is Labor's greatest asset", *The Sydney Morning Herald*, 26 April 2023.

8 "It is 1977": Yunupingu, "Tradition, truth and tomorrow", *The Monthly*, December 2008–January 2009.

8 "came to inform" and "did not undertake": *Petitions of the Aboriginal People of Yirrkala*, 14 August and 28 August 1963.

9 "Mapoon people have remained strong": *Final Report of the Referendum Council*, p. 19.

9 "What I see now": Mick Dodson, quoted in David Brearley and David Nason, "The long division: When can black and white Australia expect to be reconciled?", *Weekend Australian*, 24–25 October 1998.

10 "In the first recommendation": Patricia Anderson and Rex Wild, *Ampe Akelyernemane Meke Mekarle, "Little Children Are Sacred": Report of the Northern Territory Board of Inquiry into the Protection of Aboriginal Children from Sexual Abuse*, Northern Territory Government, 2007, p. 21.

10 "what is first said", "ongoing process", "represent all members": *Little Children Are Sacred*, p. 52.

10–11 "indigenous peoples' power": Kim Carr, quoted in "ATSIC abolished after bill passes parliament", *The Sydney Morning Herald*, 17 March 2005.

11 "appoint a group": John Howard, Joint Press Conference with Senator Amanda Vanstone, Parliament House, Canberra, 15 April 2004.

11 "tremendous amount of goodwill": Amanda Vanstone, quoted in "ATSIC abolished after bill passes parliament".

11 "In future, it is likely": Kerry Arabena, *Not Fit for Modern Society: Aboriginal and Torres Strait Islander people and the new arrangements for the administration of Indigenous affairs*, AIATSIS, Research Discussion Paper, No. 16, Native Title Research Unit, Canberra, 2005.

12 "regulatory ritualism": Robert Merton, *Social Theory and Social Structure*, Free Press, New York, 1968, p. 194.

12 "the acceptance of institutionalised means": John Braithwaite, Toni Makkai and Valerie Braithwaite, *Regulating Aged Care: Ritualism and the new pyramid*, Edward Elgar, London, 2007, p. 7.

14 "perplexed to discover": Megan Davis, *Family Is Culture Review Report 2019*, Independent Review of Aboriginal Children and Young People in OOC, Sydney, October 2019. p. 442.

15 "Institutions of justice": Valerie Braithwaite and Mary Ivec, "Policing child protection: Motivational postures of contesting third parties", *Asian Journal of Criminology*, vol. 17, 2022, pp. 425–48.

17 "Bureaucracy is a large beast", "As a caseworker": *Family Is Culture Review Report 2019*, pp. xxiii, xiv.

19–20 "lack of consultation", "Small organisations": Department of Prime Minister and Cabinet, *Indigenous Advancement Strategy*, Auditor-General, ANAO Report No. 35, 2016–17, pp. 23, 69.

20 "Most Australians": Noel Pearson to *The Australian*, as quoted in Megan Davis, "Gesture politics: Recognition alone won't fix Indigenous affairs", UNSW Newsroom, 10 December 2015.

21 "strategy did not reduce red tape": Department of Prime Minister and Cabinet, *Indigenous Advancement Strategy*, p. 70.

21 "bogged down in bureaucracy", "It is likely": Fred Chaney, "Is Australia big enough for reconciliation?", Speech delivered at the ANU Reconciliation Lecture, Canberra, 1 December 2014.

22 "aim is to ensure", "because AFANT was": Lorena Allam, "Indigenous advancement funding redirected to cattlemen and fishing groups", *Guardian Australia*, 31 October 2018.

23 "violated political conventions": Dylan Lino, *Constitutional Recognition: First Peoples and the Australian settler state*, The Federation Press, Leichhardt, 2018, p. 36.

24 "We will be asking": Gatjil Djerrkura, "Retreat from rights", *The Australian*, 3 January 1998.

24 "off-loaded": Michael Dillon, *The First Decade of Closing the Gap: What went wrong?* Centre for Aboriginal Economic Policy Research Discussion Paper 298/2021, ANU College of Arts & Social Sciences, 2021.

24 "Despite the popular conception": Julian Leeser, "Community input must be at the heart of the Voice process", *The Australian*, 20 January 2021.

25 "to the maximum extent possible", "fiscal federalism driver", etc.: Dillon, *The First Decade of Closing the Gap*.

25 "has no intention": Michael Dillon, *The New Policy Architecture for Closing the Gap: Innovation and regression*, Discussion Paper No 298/2021, Centre for Aboriginal Economic Policy Research, Australian National University, 2021, p. 13.

25 "effectively abandoned": Chris Holland, *Close the Gap: 10 year review*, Close the Gap Campaign Steering Committee, 2018, pp. 4, 8 and 22.

25 "implementation fell away", "federal–state cooperation," "leveraging of mainstream funding", and "the key oversight and implementation": Joint Council on Closing the Gap, *Review of the National Indigenous Reform Agreement (NIRA)*, Adelaide, 23 August 2019, pp. 2, 3, 4 and 5.

26 "This strategy has been pursued": Dillon, *The First Decade of Closing the Gap*, p. 11.

27 "their minds": Yunupingu, "Tradition, truth and tomorrow".

29 "Frank supports": Noel Pearson, Joint Select Committee on the Aboriginal and Torres Strait Islander Voice Referendum, *Hansard*, Canberra, 1 May 2023.

29 "even the most hateful": Miranda Fricker, *Epistemic Injustice: Power and the ethics of knowing*, Oxford University Press, Oxford, 2007, p. 26.

30 "unfinished business": Patrick Dodson, "Beyond the Mourning Gate", AIATSIS, 12 May 2000.

30 "Those societies": Andrew Fitzmaurice, *Sovereignty, Property and Empire 1500–2000*, Cambridge University Press, 2014, p. 31.

32 "It provided", "Like it or not": Paul McHugh, *Aboriginal Societies and the Common Law: A history of sovereignty, status and self-determination*, Oxford University Press, Oxford, 2005, p. 4.

33 "The basis of settlement": Referendum Council, *Discussion Paper on Constitutional Recognition of Aboriginal and Torres Strait Islander People*, October 2016, p. 4.

33 "observe the genius", "You are also", "to endeavour": British Admiralty, Secret Instruction Book, in J.M. Bennett and A.C. Castles, *A Source Book of Australian Legal History: Source materials from the eighteenth to the twentieth centuries*, Law Book Co., Sydney, 1979, pp. 253–4.

35 "In the early months": Thom Blake, *A Dumping Ground: A history of the Cherbourg settlement*, University of Queensland Press, St Lucia, 2001.

35 "memories of class rule" and "In the self-governing Australasian colonies": Marilyn Lake, *Progressive New World: How settler colonialism and transpacific exchange shaped American reform*, Cambridge, Massachusetts, Harvard University Press, 2019.

36 "Historians often tell it", etc.: Ann Curthoys and Jessie Mitchell, *Taking Liberty: Indigenous rights and settler self government in colonial Australia, 1830–1890*, Cambridge University Press, 28 September 2018.

36 "progressive reforms": Lake, *Progressive New World*.

36 "the supposed mundanity": Curthoys and Mitchell, *Taking Liberty*, p. 2.

37 "From the oral histories": Noel Pearson, *A Rightful Place: Race, recognition and a more complete Commonwealth*, Quarterly Essay 55, 2014.

38 "it is precisely": Miguel Alfonso Martinez, *Study on Treaties, Agreements and Other Constructive Arrangements Between States and Indigenous Populations: Final report*, United Nations, 22 June 1999.

38 "Britain actually was the only colonial power": Martinez, *Study on Treaties*.

39 "The processes": Stephen Young and Harry Hobbs, "Modern treaty making and the limits of the law", *University of Toronto Law Journal*, vol. 71, 2021.

40 "On 5 June": Stuart Rintoul, *Lowitja: The authorised biography of Lowitja O'Donoghue*, Allen & Unwin, 2020, p. 214.

41 "They seek to achieve": James Cockayne, "More than sorry: Constructing a legal architecture for practical reconciliation", *Sydney Law Review*, vol. 23, no. 4, 2001, pp. 577–8.

41 "invite the deep consideration", "with structural political change": Charlotte Lloyd, *Managing Indigeneity, Cultivating Citizens: Reconciliation Action Plans in Australian organizations*, PhD thesis, Harvard University, 2019, p. 44.

42 "encourage organizations", "positions Indigenous difference": Lloyd, *Managing Indigeneity*, p. 161.

46 "Any reform": Megan Davis, "Constitutional recognition for Indigenous Australians must involve structural change", UNSW Newsroom, 18 February 2020.

47 "Hope, on one hand": Walter Brueggemann, *The Prophetic Imagination*, Fortress Press, 2001, p. 110.

48 "if what we know": Hans Vaihinger, *The Philosophy of "As If": A system of the theoretical, practical and religious fictions of mankind*, trans. C. K. Ogden. London: Routledge, 2009 [1911].

48 "it is a gentle jeremiad": Kwame Anthony Appiah, *As If: Idealization and ideals*, Harvard University Press, Cambridge, 2017.

48 "ethical loneliness", etc.: Jill Stauffer, *Ethical Loneliness: The injustice of not being heard*, Columbia University Press, 2015, p. 21.

51 "flowing among and through us" and "Contrast this": David Bohm, *On Dialogue*, Routledge, 1996, pp. 5–7.

53 "The Dialogue process": *Final Report of the Referendum Council*, p. 10.

54 "in which": Bohm, *On Dialogue*, p. 7.

54 "What sense did it make": Megan Davis, 2021 Mabo Oration, AIATSIS Summit, Adelaide.

57 "The logic": *Final Report of the Referendum Council*, p.14.

59 "Government can transform": *Report of the Royal Commission into Aboriginal Deaths in Custody*, 15 April 1991, section 27.9.2.

61 "It just seems to me", etc.: Bret Walker, *Hansard*, Joint Select Committee on the Aboriginal and Torres Strait Islander Voice Referendum, Inquiry into the Aboriginal and Torres Strait Islander Voice Referendum, Canberra, 14 April 2023, pp. 39, 40.

65 "What Aboriginal people ask": Yunupingu, "Rom Watangu", *The Monthly*, July 2016.

66 "Sometimes": Hans Vaihinger, 'Preface' to Appiah, *As If*, p. xii.

THE WIRES THAT BIND

Correspondence

Simon Holmes à Court

Some say the energy transition – decarbonising our energy: that is, what we must do to hold on to a liveable climate – is the biggest transformation since the industrial revolution. This greatly overstates the task, and makes it sound much scarier than it really is.

Saul Griffith has a knack for simplifying what others tend to complicate: decarbonising Australia is largely a matter of us replacing 101 million machines that rely on fire with ones that don't. As Saul says, we need to "carry out the fire." Thanks, Prometheus, electricity will take it from here!

As we replace fire with electrons, it is of course critical that we use "green" electrons … or rather, electricity produced by non-polluting sources. And here Australia is doing pretty well. Twelve years ago, just 9 per cent of our electricity came from renewable sources – mainly hydro, with a smattering of wind, solar and bioenergy. Renewables sit at 36 per cent today, with solar in front, wind close behind and hydro and bioenergy unchanged. In the scenario the Australian Energy Market Operator currently deems most likely, renewables provide 90 per cent of the energy in a significantly larger grid just twelve years from now, and 98 per cent a decade later.

That future is not "in the bag," but the engineering, economic and political momentums are all pulling decisively in that direction. There's a lot of policy work, investment and construction to ensure we get there at the lowest cost, but energy experts almost unanimously agree that this decarbonisation of our *supply* side is inevitable.

Saul has done a great service by shining a light on the energy *demand* side – the vast majority of the 101 million "fire" machines belong to punters, in their homes and driveways.

The punters are going to replace pretty much all their machines over the next decade or two as the machines age. What's critical is that the old "fire" machines are replaced by machines of decarbonisation – air conditioners instead of gas space heaters, heat pumps instead of gas water heaters, induction instead of gas stoves and cars powered by batteries instead of petrol.

If it is done right, most people won't notice the decarbonisation of our energy system. Our rooms will be illuminated, our showers will continue to be steaming hot and our houses will be no less comfortable whether it's searing hot or freezing cold outside. Few will stop to consider that the power now comes mostly from wind and solar rather than from burning coal and gas and dumping carbon dioxide and other pollutants into the air – using the atmosphere as a giant open sewer, as Al Gore likes to put it.

In this inevitable future, those who drive will enjoy better cars – cleaner, quieter and zippier – but their wheels will no longer be driven by a couple of hundred small explosions of petroleum a second under the bonnet.

As Saul rightly points out, households will save thousands from their budgets by making the switch.

The elephant in the room is that many of these "fire-less" machines currently cost more to buy than the ones we've been buying for decades. Even though the lifetime costs are lower, or soon will be, what matters to most households is the cost today.

Unfortunately, if your gas hot water system dies today, chances are your plumber will replace it with another gas burner, locking in another two decades of emissions. Anyone replacing an internal combustion engine car today is more than likely to purchase another petrol burner, again locking in another two decades of emissions. In both cases, you'll also be locking in two decades of higher energy costs.

Thankfully, we can draw on our own experience to solve this problem. In 2002, just 253 households in Australia installed solar panels. Costs were very high. For some of these early adopters, it would have been an economic decision – for example, a remote household that otherwise would have relied on diesel generation for all its power. It's likely that other households were enthusiasts who just wanted to play with a new technology, but neither scenario could be considered the mainstream.

Early on, the subsidies were massive: up to $8000 per kilowatt. Nowadays, the subsidies are much smaller, less than $400 per kilowatt and falling. Thanks to the falling cost of solar and a strong value proposition, almost 290,000 households installed solar last year and now more than one-third of Australian homes have an array on the roof. Solar is now truly mainstream – most of these households didn't install solar to save emissions; their motivation was to save money.

Australians love technology and will flock to it if it's readily available and they can justify the investment.

We now need to ensure that the machines of decarbonisation are also readily available and make financial sense to the mainstream household. This is not a call for subsidies, but for smarter, friction-free financing. Take $10,000 off the cost of a new electric vehicle at the point of purchase, and recoup the program cost through annual registration fees. Discount heat-pump hot water systems at the point of purchase, but recoup the costs of the discount through (lower) energy bills. In both cases consumers will be better off, and society will be closer to meeting its decarbonisation goals.

I'm reminded of Emma Marris's important *New York Times* piece "How to Stop Freaking Out and Tackle Climate Change," in which she implored us to stop thinking of personal sacrifice as a solution to climate change – that won't achieve much, if anything. Rather, we need to focus on systemic change, work to build movements in our communities, elect the right people and pass the right laws. When doing the right thing – the thing that needs to be done – is the easiest thing, even the totally disengaged will do their bit to decarbonise Australia.

Australians are ready to do more for decarbonisation. We just need to ensure our representatives deliver the systems to make it easy for us all to do the right thing. It's not a dichotomy between household and government action, but rather a collaboration between the two – a new, transformative social contract.

Simon Holmes à Court

Correspondence

David Pocock

Change is often hard. The renowned twentieth-century inventor Buckminster Fuller said, "You never change things by fighting the existing reality. To change something, build a new model that makes the existing model obsolete." The genius of Saul Griffith's vision is that it doesn't seek to destroy or detract from what Australians know and love. He departs from the notion that the only way to improve our energy use is to use less. Instead, he proposes a more democratic energy system that provides cheaper, more reliable and more secure energy to Australian households and businesses. All while avoiding the damage to our health, climate and economy caused by burning fossil fuels.

The scale of the change warrants feeling daunted and despairing at times. Just a week before the release of *The Wires That Bind*, the international scientific community issued another stark warning. The Intergovernmental Panel on Climate Change's Synthesis Report, described as a "survival guide to humanity," is the most reviewed document in human history. The message from scientists is as clear as it is unsurprising: we must act now: catastrophe is just around the corner. It's easy to hear this warning and feel frustrated. Many Australians have been listening to our leading scientists say the same thing for decades. We know we're embarking on this enormous task to reduce the damage to our climate at the eleventh hour.

It's easy to find reasons for the lack of long-term vision and leadership in Australian politics – the 24-hour news cycle, social media, three-year election cycles, the list goes on. And we've all suffered as a result. Many of our leaders have been happy to be weathervanes on issues, rather than articulating a vision and making decisions in the best interests of all Australians and our long-term future. Others have incited culture wars and constructed straw-man arguments when political winds start to blow in a direction that doesn't suit them or their donors. This culminated in the Morrison government arguing it didn't even have a duty to protect Australian children from the harms of climate change.

But the fact that we are starting from behind is not a reason to lose hope. It is the reason to move faster. A benefit in starting late is that we can learn from the experiences of others. Saul brings precisely this kind of experience, having had significant involvement with the US *Inflation Reduction Act*. In Australia, we can move faster by avoiding the mistakes of others, adopting models proven to succeed and rolling them out at pace and at scale.

Reducing emissions is not the only reason to increase the speed of electrification. The changes Saul proposes would also bring substantial cost-of-living relief. On his calculations, households that make the switch will save upwards of $3000 a year, every year. The key to unlocking savings is for governments to provide affordable, accessible finance and remove the regulatory hurdles that stand in the way of electrification. Public finance is already provided in many areas where public good is identified – infrastructure and higher education are prominent examples. Applying this to household electrification would allow many households to afford the upfront cost and then use the cost savings to pay back the loans and still benefit from electrification. Governments must also be careful to ensure that finance is available to everyone, regardless of their circumstances. A model for this already exists in the way that HECS is structured. This could be adopted and modified to increase the speed of electrification.

But incentives and access to affordable finance will not work for everyone, and we must ensure no one is left behind. The benefits of electrification must extend to renters, people living in apartments and people in social housing. If we get this right, the greatest benefits of electrification will flow to those in our low-income households, who spend a higher proportion of their income on energy bills and suffer more from the health and wellbeing issues that come from energy poverty.

The "miracle of rooftop solar" is a model of what is possible if we get the settings right. A combination of government investment, rebate schemes for early adopters and improving regulations to streamline the installation and accreditation process has led to us having some of the cheapest rooftop solar in the world. The scheme has had bipartisan support since John Howard introduced the photovoltaic rebate program in 2000. Politicians know that cheaper energy is a vote-winner.

The political realisation that electrification will reduce energy costs is coming. But at this point, as is so often the case, the electorate is ahead of governments. Our communities see the Australian solar miracle and understand that electrification can build on that success. In *The Wires That Bind*, Saul describes the impressive work of Electrify 2515, a community campaign to increase the speed of electrification in neighbourhoods north of Wollongong. And we're seeing groups pop up elsewhere. A passionate group of Canberrans has formed Suburb Zero to push for faster and more ambitious electrification in the ACT. The Suburb Zero campaign was launched on a Friday evening in mid-April in a packed theatre of more than 600 people. The organisers are a diverse mix of energy experts, community advocates, parents, neighbours and friends. They have been collecting surveys, door-knocking, letter-boxing thousands of houses, setting up stalls, putting up posters and talking to their friends and colleagues.

The work of groups such as Electrify 2515 and Suburb Zero shows the best in our democracy and the desire Australians have to step up and make the most of this opportunity. The suburb-wide pilot projects they're advocating provide an opportunity to increase the speed at which we find solutions to technical and regulatory issues that will inevitably arise. Successful pilots would serve as proofs of concept and inspire suburbs and regional towns across the country to electrify.

We're seeing the politics of climate change shift rapidly. People in communities across the country are realising that the challenge of decarbonising our economy presents households with huge opportunities. But even now, with climate action on the agenda at all levels of government, we're going to have to keep ratcheting up our ambition, set big goals and go faster than is comfortable. There is always risk in change, but the risks we face if we fail to seize this opportunity to transform our energy systems and decarbonise our economy mean we have little choice. *The Wires That Bind* shows us the power of collective action. Households can make a difference when it comes to reducing our emissions, but we need political leadership to remove obstacles, help scale that effort and install the right policy settings for the rest of our economy.

Saul Griffith shows how electrification can help address two of the most pressing challenges we face: climate change and the cost of living. The opportunity is here. We can make this happen.

David Pocock

Correspondence

Christine Milne

I love the idea of electrifying everything and turning off the blue flames of fossil fuels in factories, power stations and households as rapidly as possible – for all the reasons Saul Griffith sets out. His commitment to addressing global heating, his enthusiasm for stopping burning things, his stories of community commitment and his powerful arguments underpinned by careful calculation are compelling and inspiring. Reducing greenhouse gases, better air quality, improved health, better energy security, cheaper energy, a more sustainable built environment from replacing 101 million machines with new, more efficient, better and more climate-friendly machines – what's not to like?

But I would have liked Saul to address the question of whether we can afford it, if the shift from fossil fuels to renewable energy destroys ecosystems? Can the Earth afford the transition to renewables if it is embedded in the linear business-as-usual, take-make-dispose model of unlimited consumerism and economic growth? There cannot be infinite growth on a finite planet. Without that recognition as the foundation, electrifying everything will boost economic growth and consumerism (with a green salve) while continuing to destroy biodiversity, extract resources and dump waste, in largely hidden practices.

How effective is the electric transformation if there are three Teslas and a heavy electric truck in the renovated garage? If we do not "internalise the externalities" of the resource extraction needed to produce these vehicles, or the new transmission infrastructure to convey that electricity, it will be a recipe for community conflict. Already, mines such as that proposed by Venture Minerals in the Tarkine forest are justified on the basis that boron is "an important and versatile element in the modern world, used in everything from computer screens to fertilisers to creating powerful magnets for wind turbines and EVs (electric vehicles)."

Gangs on the streets of Brisbane and Sydney are stealing catalytic converters from the exhaust systems of our petrol fleet to recover precious minerals such as platinum, while governments don't bother to recycle cars or whitegoods to recover metals and rare minerals and instead send them for waste disposal and approve new mines. The failure to manage waste from the technological revolution is evident in the mountains of e-waste that pile up or are exported. What will happen to 20 million cars and gas burners over a decade?

Saul has started charting a critical path. As we walk it, we must keep in mind that climate and biodiversity are two sides of the same coin. We cannot destroy one in the name of the other. Electrification has to occur within ecosystem limits, not by "offsetting" or ignoring or trashing these limits.

But this is possible. At the end of his essay, Saul argues that "we can show the world later this century what a circular economy really looks like."

In a linear economy, to quote an online reference, "raw materials are retrieved and made into products that are used until they are discarded as waste. This economic system relies on selling as many products as possible," even when there is a focus on "eco-efficiency," or minimising the ecological impact to get the same output.

By contrast, a circular economy focuses on reducing, reusing and recycling. "Resource use is minimised (reduce). Reuse of products and parts is maximized (reuse). And last but not least, raw materials are reused (recycled) to a high standard. This can be done by using goods with more people, such as shared cars. Products can also be converted into services, such as [the way] Spotify sells listening licences instead of CDs. In this system, value is created by focusing on value preservation ... This means that not only the ecological impact is minimized, but that the ecological, economic and social impact is even positive."

We can advocate energy efficiency and, as Saul outlines, pull government levers to constrain demand, meet supply, change consumer attitudes and prompt innovation within existing development footprints. Sulphur batteries, for example, don't need scarce resources such as cobalt. Fuel efficiency standards, building standards, EV targets, sunset dates for fossil-fuel machines or weight-based road charges, separate bike lanes and removal of electric-bike power limits, community-based feed-in tariffs – all these should be part of a government plan to complement individual and community plans. But we need to acknowledge that ultimately we must pull those levers in a circular economy which is not divorced from local biodiversity and waste streams. How much better to have a distributed rooftop solar generator than to destroy a forest or unique ecosystem? How much better to protect a forest and recover metals and minerals from obsolete machines rather than dig a new mine?

Reducing demand for metals and minerals and land for new generation, along with establishing facilities to recover and recycle resources – this is what must be installed as the Electrify Everything transformation gets underway. Once the energy transformation is embedded in the linear economy and runs parallel to the fossil-fuel economy, it will be almost impossible to retrofit. The country will have lost the jobs and social and environmental benefits of cradle-to-grave resource recovery, better urban design opportunities from electrification of the transport fleet, and it will have torn itself apart. Communities are already becoming polarised and conflict-ridden over congested cities, overcrowded parking areas, resource extraction, mines, land alienation, transmission and biodiversity impacts consequent upon the existing transition – let alone before we become a renewable energy "Superpower" supplying energy to meet overseas demands as well as our own. Yet we have a great opportunity to embed circular principles now, and we must do so to maintain ecosystems, community cohesion and the social licence for renewable energy.

To be a truly transforming force, Electrify Everything has to be more than a politically safe, siloed, clean-energy initiative; it must repudiate the discourse of delay that has overtaken Australian politics. We have shifted from a "fossil-fuel only" economy to a "let's have it both ways" economy. Let's maintain fossil fuels and delay the transition for as long as we can, but at the same time, in parallel, create new businesses and exports from a clean economy sector and facilitate them both with "offsets." It is a deliberate and successful "divide and rule" strategy to smother dissent from the climate activist community. It is an economic growth strategy based on exporting fossil fuels and building clean energy infrastructure as if the two were completely compatible. It is a "something for everyone" climate and energy strategy.

Many who argue for the transition to renewables deliberately avoid hard-edged condemnation of the delay discourse to maintain political access. Embracing technological optimism and a "carrots, not sticks" approach sits as happily with Woodside as it does with climate investor groups. The "just pass it" mentality that drove the 43 per cent emissions reduction target and the Safeguard Mechanism is the politics of delay.

Saul notes the way government and regulatory bodies such as the AEMO have, in recent years, maintained the status quo and delayed the transformation from fossil fuels to renewable energy. But he doesn't take the next step and call for the complete clean-out of these bodies. I do. We are entering a period of chaos, greenwashing and bad decisions because the regulatory authorities are not up to the challenge and are committed to business as usual.

Christine Milne

Correspondence

Ian McAuley

Opponents of meaningful action on climate change present households as powerless victims, financially crippled by ever-increasing electricity bills, threatened by blackouts when the sun doesn't shine and the wind doesn't blow, and faced with the terrifying prospect of the $100 roast.

Saul Griffith's essay dispels this fog of misinformation. Households aren't just passive consumers. Rather, they can join in the task of energy transformation, a transformation that, far from requiring sacrifice, offers expansive possibilities. As we move to full electrification, fed by abundant renewable resources, not only will we enjoy lower prices but we will also be participants in community renewal, because that transformation, in changing the way energy is produced and distributed, will result in social developments in a way that previous waves of technology have done.

Griffith's main contribution is to apply the hard discipline of engineering to develop an economically and financially realistic way for that vision to be achieved, starting with the practicalities of what to do when your gas water heater or cooktop is due for replacement.

Most engineers, when talking about energy systems, start at the generation end and work from there to the three-pin plug on your wall. In a class or a public lecture their first slide or drawing will be of a power station – perhaps a 1- or 2-GW coal-fired power station, or more recently a large solar array or wind farm. They will then move to the high-voltage transmission lines that deliver electricity around the country, the transformers and low-voltage lines that distribute electricity around cities, and finally the 240-volt line that brings electricity into your house.

Griffith covers all these elements but in reverse order: he starts with your lightbulb (LED, of course), cooktop (induction) or car (electric), and builds from there to the generator, not necessarily to a large power station or a big battery, but possibly to some community-based network of small-scale generators and batteries.

It's not that he ignores the need for big pieces of infrastructure, such as high-voltage transmission lines connecting our geographically and time-zone separated renewable energy hot spots, or big batteries, such as the Snowy 2.0 "battery" with a short-term power output (2 GW) that matches that of our largest coal-fired stations. We need these big pieces of infrastructure, but rather than being at the core of our energy supply, their role will be complementary to a system where the conversion of sun and wind energy to electricity is increasingly in small-scale units, ranging from household rooftop solar to small-scale cooperative ventures.

As for storage, to provide electricity when the sun doesn't shine and the wind doesn't blow, particularly during the early evening peak, there's the battery on wheels: the electric car.

One may wonder why Griffith is so concerned with the household. A glance at Australia's energy statistics reveals that households use only 28 per cent of electricity and 10 per cent of gas produced for the domestic market. But there are three reasons why these figures understate the importance of households.

First, they do not include households' use of energy in their cars, which dwarfs our consumption of energy for other purposes. With better urban design we may use our cars less in the future, but we will still use them, a point he illustrates in the essay itself, much of which he wrote while on an electric-car road trip.

In the short term, we can make significant savings to our household budgets and to the nation's contribution to emissions through investing in heat pumps, electric cooktops and insulation, but in time we will be using much more electricity to power our cars. If we get it right, much of that electricity will be generated locally, from panels on our roofs or in car parks.

Second is the nature of household demand. Much industrial and commercial demand corresponds with times when renewable energy is plentiful, and some energy-intensive industrial processes, even aluminium smelting, can shape their usage accordingly. For such big users the spot market works well. But households do not have easily changeable habits. We cook in the early evening and turn on heaters when it gets chilly in the evening. Add an electric car into this mix, plugging in to recharge when arriving home from work, and the problem is exacerbated.

This peak demand drives the case for gas-fired peaking power stations, and is even used by defenders of fossil-fuel generators to argue for 24/7 "dispatchable" or even "baseload" power. These old power stations, with their massive spinning inertia, were wasteful but they were magnificently shockproof to events such as everybody turning on their hot water jugs in an ad break during *Neighbours*.

Catering for peaks with fossil-fuel generators is high cost. Having this supply available has therefore had a strong influence on the price of electricity. Ideally, if demand could be shaped in line with potential supply from low-cost renewable sources, we could get the price of electricity down towards 4 cents per kWh, the cost of rooftop solar, compared with the 28 cents we are paying now. That would be unachievable, but as a practical solution, Griffith shows that with the help of batteries we can get the cost down to 12 to 15 cents.

That is why he stresses the need for every household to have a Home Energy Management System (HEMS), "a dorky acronym for the computer that will manage all the flows of electrons between the things in your life." Your HEMS will turn on your washing machine and dishwasher around the middle of the day when renewable energy is cheap. It will heat your well-insulated hot water system when there are short periods of strong winds driving wind farms. In so doing it not only saves you money, it also benefits all users who do not have to pay so much for peak supply.

The third reason to emphasise households is political. Griffith's essay is largely about the political economy of our energy transformation and he describes how households have been used in the weaponisation of arguments around renewable energy. Large industrial and commercial users of energy, some of which bypass the energy "retailers," can handle the energy transition well. They use the same analysis as Griffith does to understand the value in upgrading their installations. But for households it's different. Even though many investments in upgrading appliances are so attractive that they could justifiably be financed at credit-card interest rates, many people just can't get their hands on $700 for a new refrigerator or $1000 for a heat pump to replace their gas heater and electric radiators. Also, in the rental market there are particular problems impeding energy-saving investments.

Furthermore, as behavioural economists know, even those with access to cash are prone to making poor investment decisions, psychologically overestimating the burden of immediate outlays while underestimating the benefits of future savings.

Griffith deals with the problem of access to credit, citing a scheme already in place in New South Wales. The harder problem lies not only in that short-term bias recognised by behavioural economists but also in people's general disengagement from anything to do with electricity and gas.

In fact, the very notion of householders exercising agency in energy use seems to be alien to those who speak and write about electricity. Last year's budget papers, for example, forecast a 56 per cent rise in electricity prices, which many journalists reported as an increase of 56 per cent in electricity bills, as if households have no control over their energy use.

Many people (apart from retired engineers) find it difficult to engage with electricity. They may know the price of a litre of petrol, maybe even their car's fuel consumption per 100 kilometres, while being stumped when it comes to the price per kWh of electricity or the annual usage of their refrigerator. They may not even know what a kWh is, let alone a megajoule of gas.

The public aren't helped by the opaque and clunky technology in electricity metering and billing, or by media and government statements asserting that a certain policy change will save or cost consumers $X year, without expressing that in terms of cents per kWh – as Griffith does so carefully in his essay.

There is ample evidence that households want to do their part in combating climate change, but they need basic knowledge if they are to take meaningful steps – not to worry about the light left on or the standby power for their television, but to go for the big gains in the way they choose and use electrical machines and appliances.

Griffith's vision involves households and communities becoming active participants, rather than passive consumers, in our energy transformation. That's hardly radical: three million households already have panels on their roofs.

His vision, however, is unsettling for economists schooled in the idea that supply and demand have their separate existences, represented by their respective lines intersecting at a neatly defined price. Economists see household production as a relic of a pre-industrial era that can be safely ignored in their models.

As an engineer, Griffith understands energy in a way that economists do not. It's not simply that he knows about the technologies and their cost functions (which rarely resemble an economist's supply curve). He also applies the basic discipline of engineering to describe an interactively complex and dynamic system. Furthermore, he is an advocate – an advocate for a world in which we can reduce emissions while enjoying an enriched lifestyle. His is practical advocacy, based on evidence rather than the imagined benefits of privatisation and structural separation that have shaped the National Electricity Market.

Ian McAuley

Rebecca Huntley

Public attitudes to the electrification of our domestic energy market have changed dramatically since I started in-depth research on Australian perceptions about climate change and energy transformation around five years ago.

When it comes to transport, any widespread fears that electric cars would destroy the great Australian weekend seem to have diminished. (I doubt they were ever widespread, to be honest, given most Australian weekends involve driving to IKEA, where there will soon be free charging stations.) Research conducted in 2021 by the Electric Vehicle Council found 54 per cent of Australians would consider purchasing an electric vehicle as their next car and 49 per cent could see themselves in an EV by 2030. The Australia Institute's annual Climate of the Nation report in 2022 showed that 76 per cent of Australians rank solar in their top three preferred energy sources, compared to 17 per cent for coal, 21 per cent for gas and 22 per cent for nuclear. The research I work on with the Sunrise Project, Climate Compass, shows that that 43 per cent of Australians are open to replacing their gas appliances with electric.

Saul Griffith's Quarterly Essay lays out in simple and compelling terms the pathway for electrification. He helps us understand how we can play a role in action on climate because, as he states at the outset, we can't wait for others (government, corporations and so on) to act. We can and must act in our own homes and communities. In saying so, he taps into what social research shows is one of the main barriers to action for most of us: "I want to act but I don't know what would make the biggest impact."

I am not a policy wonk but a social researcher interested in both community attitudes to fossil-fuel use as well as the social conditions required for greater ambition when it comes to climate action and energy transition. And so I am interested in the attention he gives to "the new social contract" required so that every Australian can "join the game."

Right now, it is undeniably a game without a level playing field, which Griffith acknowledges throughout his essay. In my own research, I find people on low incomes, renters and those who own homes that can't accommodate off-street parking or don't have a flat, sunny roof talk about aspiring to solar panels, a heat pump, an EV but don't know what might make that happen. More renewable energy infrastructure, more government support, more accessible consumer choices, more leverage with real estate agents – all of these are needed. As is addressing the structural barriers locking First Nations communities out of renewable energy and energy-efficiency solutions. These communities are managing the dual challenge of fighting fossil-fuel companies on issues such as fracking and fighting for a seat at the table when it comes to large-scale renewable energy projects on or close to Country.

Griffith talks about the almost magical capacity that electrification, done right, has – not only to give us cheaper, cleaner energy, but also to realign some of the vectors of power (economic and political) that crisscross this sunburnt country. He describes this shared vision in visionary terms: "We can renew our communities, local and national, through electrification and replacing fossil-fuel-burning cars and appliances with ones powered by clean energy. We need to do this to conserve our world, but it also brings other benefits, not least of which are financial, and the best of which is creating wires that bind us to our neighbours and to each other as Australians." It's a vision the people in the focus groups I conduct would love to believe in. Some are on the way to being persuaded. Others need further proof of concept.

Griffith's endearing travels with his mother on his book tour rightly highlight the capacity of women to create a well-lit, well-resourced, more connected country. The data that shows more women than men are alarmed and active on climate. From the climate strikers to the Teal independents to the powerhouses in the Country Women's Associations and Rotary Clubs. Griffith is also using the right kind of language when he describes electrification as a "retrofit" and "replace" agenda. "Every time a dirty fossil machine breaks, we need to replace it with a clean one." That's useful terminology when you are communicating with more conservative, older men, those who are far more sceptical about our role in climate change. Practical, cheaper, cleaner: that's speaking their language.

In Australia, Griffith's work has been influential with the new wave of independents, helping them push both Labor and the LNP, and therefore the national politics. This is essential. And indeed, while there is much we can all do as consumers, in our workplaces and households, there are limits. The social research shows that two of the key barriers to greater action on climate and energy transition across all groups of Australians are "it is too hard" and "I already do a lot for the environment." There is a danger in placing too much emphasis on consumer choice and household decision-making (which inevitably puts a lot of pressure on low-income households and women). With the ALP in control federally and in every state and territory (bar Tasmania, which has already made a commitment to 200 per cent renewable energy by 2040), the key to success is finding a way to support the Labor agenda while encouraging greater ambition through better engagement with unions and important groups such as the Labor Environmental Action Network. Without systems change in the party that makes the decisions about how to power this country, we risk a renewable-energy divide developing, with some suburbs full of EVs and heat pumps and others full of old tech, rising energy costs and resentment.

Rebecca Huntley

THE WIRES THAT BIND

Correspondence

Bjorn Sturmberg

While the pivotal role of electrification in decarbonisation has been understood for decades, it has rarely been described as vividly or enthusiastically as by Saul Griffith in *The Wires That Bind*. Griffith recognises that electrification is a story, at its heart, not about decarbonisation but about cleaning the air in our kitchens and streets, improving the liveability of our homes and communities, and "keeping wealth in our households and communities" – and nation. In short, electrification is a story about a better future.

While attuned to this human story of electrification, Griffith is, at heart, an engineer so it's no surprise that *The Wires That Bind* is packed full of figures. Emissions are carved up, the grid is mapped and fossil-fuel machines are counted. This achieves Griffith's goal of "clarity about the job in front of us" and complements his persuasive case for electrifying everything. The question that remains is: how can the transition best be accelerated and steered towards just and enduring outcomes?

Part of the answer is the substitution of fossil-fuel machines with electric machines and subsidies to expedite this, as advocated by Griffith and Rewiring Australia. But these substitutions are insufficient (and oddly conservative, given Griffith's reputation for out-there ideas). What's more, while straight substitution has fuelled the fastest transitions in history, it has invariably led to new, sometimes worse, problems. The example given of cars replacing horses (which was also motivated by a pollution problem – that originating from horses' backsides) is a salient example: cars went on to drive global warming, respiratory diseases, obesity, road accidents, social isolation and the mass consumption of resources and real estate. As Griffith points out, the substitution of our fossil-fuel cars with electric Hummers could exacerbate more of these harms.

So how else can the transition be effected? My research suggests four interrelated approaches: (re)building trust, focusing on collective values over individual responsibility, reducing demand, and empowering a broader set of stakeholders.

First and foremost, we need to move beyond our myopic focus on markets and machines to instead focus on trust – not technology or taxes. For, as Chilli Heeler explained it to her daughters Bluey and Bingo, "if there's no trust, none of this [the world] is possible ... No libraries, no roads, no power lines."

Markets don't foster trust. Market mechanisms, such as evening peak pricing, have not changed when families eat – nor should they. Their greatest success has been to send pensioners to bed at 4 p.m. to shiver under blankets instead of running their heaters. *The Wires That Bind* plots how twenty-five years of energy-sector privatisation in Australia has fuelled hyper-inflation of prices. What's harder to plot and harder yet to undo is the consequent hyperdeflation of trust in the sector.

To give just one example of a non-market initiative that would earn back trust, governments (or the energy sector) could provide households with a cost-free energy allowance to cover their essential needs, including refrigeration and cooking. An elegant model could link this consumption with government-owned renewables generation.

Technology, likewise, neither creates trust nor replaces it. The rise of cryptocurrency scams and collapses is a timely reminder that we need to trust the humans on the other end of algorithms. For the energy sector, this should temper visions of trustless, blockchain-facilitated peer-to-peer trading and the Home Energy Management Systems that Griffith presumes will become ubiquitous. Research, such as the Digital Energy Futures project, keeps finding broad rejection of smart technologies and tariff-based incentives: people prefer hands-on control and to shift their demand by shifting routines.

The second approach, which also works towards building trust, switches the focus from individual responsibility (as a market participant or climate citizen) to collective values. As Griffith puts it, "the challenges of climate change need a politics of the collective more than a politics of the individual." One way to put this into practice would be to conceive of the grid as a "common good." This points us to lessons from managing other common resources, such as water. Drought-time water reductions, for instance, are not achieved through financial contracts or automated tap-closing devices but through social contracts of solidarity. Temporary electricity demand reductions, which are invaluable during periods of low renewables generation or peak demand, could be pursued through similar means.

Rooftop solar systems could be monitored in the way rural fire brigades monitor their community's water tanks and dams. These solar systems today have greater combined power capacity than the biggest generator in the country – they are truly, as Griffith notes, critical national infrastructure. But there are no processes in place for monitoring their performance or managing their maintenance.

This critical gap would be best filled by local or state governments, network companies or a not-for-profit, not by individuals – we don't, after all, make individuals responsible for maintaining roads or the NBN.

The commons framing also highlights the risk of "free riding," which can arise when turbulent transitions throw costs and benefits into the air. As an example, households that install solar and/or disconnect from gas are reducing their contribution to the upkeep of the electricity and gas networks without altering the total cost of maintaining these networks. This increases the burden on remaining customers, who are increasingly those facing barriers to make such upgrades. In contrast to Griffith's description, increased use of the electricity network will likewise leave the total maintenance costs unchanged, but it may alter their distribution. The huge opportunity for saving is to decommission the gas network completely.

The first step in tackling distributional questions is to define who's in and who's out of the community/commons. I strongly believe in the principle of considering communities with the greatest diversity and number of constituents. Only within broad communities can inequities be redressed. This principle runs counter to the popular trend of localism, which Griffith's suburb- and postcode-based initiatives play into, and instead emphasises the role of network companies and governments, which represent large and diverse swathes of the country. An outstanding example of this is the "postage stamp" model of paying for electricity, under which all the customers of a network pay the same price, despite the cost of serving rural customers at the end of long lines being many times greater than the cost of serving urban customers.

After personally spending years bringing solar to the roofs of apartments and rentals, I now believe the most equitable and effective approach gives these customers access to cheap and green grid electricity. Similarly, I believe there are efficiency, environmental and equity advantages to grid-scale storage, such as hydropower stations and batteries at wind farms, rather than Griffith's vision of 5 million household batteries. Grid-scale storage lets diverse customer behaviour average itself out, before responding to residual imbalances of supply and demand. This efficiency reduces the quantity of batteries required, and the shared nature of grid assets avoids inequity risks. Additionally, the need for dedicated short-term storage assets will be greatly diminished in 100 per cent renewable grids because of the abundance of long-term storage assets that have been built to cover multi-day stretches with low renewables generation.

The third approach to the energy transition is greater investment in the "demand side," which, despite representing the raison d'être of the energy system, has been overshadowed by supply-side initiatives. *The Wires That Bind* overlooks the foundational role of non-electrical ways of fulfilling human needs. Insulation, ventilation and thermal mass can create more comfortable buildings at lower carbon, material and financial costs than the latest, greatest air-conditioner. Reconfiguring urban layouts and infrastructure to place work and services within a fifteen-minute commute via active and public transport will create happier, healthy and more socially connected communities than merely swapping drivetrains. Perhaps the slogan can be elongated to "eliminate, then electrify everything"?

The defining challenge of demand-side actions is that they take place where people live and work. This raises the complexity and stakes of implementation and maintenance. Australia's unrivalled roll-out of rooftop solar provides two salient lessons in this regard. The first is that leaving implementation to the market invites what Griffiths politely describes as a "perpetual stream of 'buy solar now!' advertising," as well as some companies pursuing more predatory sales techniques and a race to the bottom on cost and quality of components and services – what industry insiders call "crap solar."

The second lesson is that social expectations and technical standards should be defined in preparation for ubiquitous uptake. This would mitigate the confusions and frustrations that have followed repeated modifications to solar system functionalities. As electric vehicle sales accelerate, our research on vehicle-to-grid technology has demonstrated how this technology, and the flexibility offered by vehicle charging in general, will be an illusion unless there is a behavioural shift from filling cars as rarely as possible to plugging electric vehicles in whenever parked.

The fourth approach is to empower a much broader set of stakeholders "within the framework of existing institutions." One aspect of this is action by nimble communities, for which *The Wires That Bind* makes an impassioned case. But while there are exciting developments in this space, I believe a just transition ultimately requires our larger institutions to earn back our trust and then to lead.

For energy-sector institutions the issues are remit and ideology. The bodies making and enforcing the rules currently see their fundamental objective as market efficiency and their sole tool as market competition. Regulation is therefore framed around containment ("ring fencing") – restricting network companies to reacting to customer actions – rather than proactive enablement. Griffith is right that the "regulatory environment is as important as the physical one" – I was taught this by incurring $120,000 of legal work to enable the first installation of a solar and storage system (costing $80,000) in an Australian apartment. "Regulatory sandboxes" are a laudable innovation but changes to regulatory governance must go deeper.

Two institutions whose role in electrification – as champions or blockers – is often overlooked are rental property managers and tradespeople. Property managers are the under-appreciated glue that holds together Australia's three million rental arrangements. With training, resourcing and culture change, they could play a potent role in planning and managing electrification upgrades (at least upon failure of existing appliances) and having these features understood and valued by property buyers and renters. Similarly, tradespeople are the boots-on-the-ground authority on whether or not (in their opinion) it is feasible to electrify, disconnect from gas, insulate and otherwise retrofit properties.

The electrification and decarbonisation transitions are lively, uncertain processes with abundant path-dependencies. We will never know precisely how to best navigate them, but the four approaches discussed here – prioritising trust over technology and taxes, governing for the common good, eliminating demand as well as electrifying it, and empowering more stakeholders – provide some direction. Taken together, they remind us that it is not the wires that bind people together, but rather the bonds of community that are materialised in the grid's wires.

Bjorn Sturmberg

THE WIRES THAT BIND

Correspondence

Ian Lowe

Saul Griffith's wonderful contribution not only spells out a clear vision of a cleaner energy future but also describes a viable pathway to get there. This is a very significant step forward.

Nearly twenty years ago, I wrote a small book for Black Inc., the publishers of Quarterly Essay. In *A Big Fix*, I said we needed "radical solutions" to the environmental crisis unfolding around us. I argued that significant change required four things. First, there needs to be discontent, without which there is no motivation for change. Second, there needs to be a vision of a better way; unless there is a clear vision, change could make things worse rather than improving the situation. Third, there needs to be a viable path from where we are now to the place we would like to reach. Finally, there needs to be commitment to follow that path, despite predictable opposition from vested interests wanting to continue outdated practices.

Discontent, an awareness that we need to change the way we produce and use energy, has been around for decades. The CSIRO and the Commission for the Future worked together thirty-five years ago on Greenhouse '88, a program to communicate what science was saying about climate change. At the time, there was broad agreement among our elected governments of the need for change. Then the fossil-fuel industries began a systematic campaign of misinformation, adopting the approach used successfully by the tobacco industry to dissuade timid politicians from action. As Griffith points out, the more subtle misinformation continues to this day, with dishonest claims about "renewable gas," the ultimate oxymoron, and the spurious need for "baseload power."

Despite these efforts, discontent has continued to expand. Six independent reports on the state of our environment, at five-year intervals, have called with increasing urgency for action to slow climate change. The election a year ago of Teal independents and Greens members in what had been seen as safe major-party seats demonstrated the level of public concern. The vision of a better way, replacing fossil-fuel electricity with renewable energy such as solar and wind, was clear thirty years ago, but there did not appear to be a viable pathway. At the time, coal-fired electricity was much cheaper than power from solar farms and large wind turbines. The technology has improved rapidly and produced amazing cost reductions. Ten years ago, world average prices were about 8 cents per kWh for gas-fired power, about 11 cents for coal-fired, 14 for wind and 35 for solar. Last year, world average prices for fossil-fuel power were about the same as ten years ago, but the average cost for wind power was 4.1 cents per kWh and for solar farms was 3.7 cents. Remarkably, the Coalition is still holding the telescope to its blind eye, now even calling for a national debate about nuclear power. The cold hard truth is that nuclear power would make no economic sense, even if we were prepared to overlook all its other problems. The world average price of power from nuclear reactors is 16 cents, four times that of wind and solar, with the only three construction projects in western Europe, all years behind schedule and billions over budget.

It now makes economic sense to phase out fossil fuels in favour of renewables with storage. That is the easy part. Griffith correctly recognises that the electricity system only accounts for about a third of our greenhouse gas emissions. To play a responsible role in the global campaign to slow climate change, we also need to tackle the emissions from transport, cooking, manufacturing, space heating and agriculture. While the last sector is the most difficult, *The Wires That Bind* develops a coherent and credible plan for using renewable electricity to meet all our other energy needs. It builds on the solid technical work in Alan Finkel's Quarterly Essay, *Getting to Zero*. Griffith is, like Finkel, an engineer, but the real strength of this new essay is its emphasis on the social factors which will determine whether a transition is possible. The failure of prohibition in the United States and the "war on drugs" everywhere should have taught us that social acceptance is essential to achieve fundamental change. It is futile to try to stop practices that the community wants to continue.

If we are going to achieve the urgently needed transition to clean energy systems, it must be based solidly on widespread understanding of the need to change and the practicality of doing so. As Figure 2 in the essay shows, while the approach by the Albanese government is light years ahead of the decade of inaction under the Coalition, it is still too timid to give us a fighting chance of keeping the increase in average global temperature below 2°C. Our leaders need to be encouraged – literally, given courage – by the community to do what is needed. As I was writing this response, the government released its policy statement about electric vehicles. It is again a significant step forward, but still well behind what most European countries are doing to accelerate the end of petroleum-fuelled vehicles.

Griffith is right to draw attention to the dishonest claims being made by fossil-fuel interests to try to prolong their businesses. Despite decades of funding, schemes for carbon capture and storage have almost all just captured public money. While it is a good thing that small amounts of gas have been replaced by hydrogen produced from solar energy, it would be better if energy were used directly, rather than being wastefully converted, and there is absolutely no prospect of hydrogen replacing more than a small fraction of the gas. We should accept the advice of the International Energy Agency: keeping the increase in average global temperature below 2°C means no new fossil-fuel projects, anywhere, ever, and the accelerated closure of existing activities.

I only noticed one small technical slip in the section on transport, where Griffith says that road damage is proportional to the square of the weight of a vehicle. The landmark study of this question concluded that the damage is more like the fourth power of the axle load, so doubling the weight increases the damage to the surface by a factor of sixteen. That means the entire road maintenance bill is essentially a huge subsidy of road freight. Cleaning up freight transport vehicles is desirable, but it would make more sense to phase out the subsidies that have effectively moved freight from rail and coastal shipping to the roads, increasing both emissions and the numbers killed in transport accidents.

I would like to have seen more emphasis on improving the efficiency of using energy. Griffith notes the inefficiency of our cars, typically weighing more than a tonne to carry a payload less than 100 kilograms. But his section on home-energy needs implicitly accepts inadequate appliance efficiency standards that allow the dumping in Australia of goods that could not legally be sold in Europe. The report on energy efficiency presented to the Howard government twenty years ago showed our emissions could be reduced by 30 per cent, just by changing to cost-effective existing technology. We should be very angry that little has been done to introduce those changes that would put more money in our pockets as well as helping to slow climate change.

Perhaps the most interesting observation in the essay is the comment about the leadership of women. Strikingly, in the 2022 election the Teal independents elected to the House of Representatives were all women, and television crosses to election-night celebrations showed that the great majority of their supporters were also women. Surveys show that women are much more likely to support strong action on climate change than men. Older men are the group most likely to think climate change is not a problem at all. Perhaps it is time for those of us who are male, pale and stale to get out of the way and let women take over the response.

Ian Lowe

THE WIRES THAT BIND

Correspondence

Robin Batterham

We are besieged by messages about how to reduce emissions, appropriately focusing on eliminating our use of fossil fuels. The stridency of the "kill coal and gas now" theme is almost omnipresent, yet the notion that this would result in chaos is rarely mentioned. When the damage that would be done if we get our decommissioning of existing assets too far out of phase with our commissioning of new assets is mentioned, it is seen as the bleating of vested interests. There is then relief in reading Saul Griffith's essay, as it acknowledges the challenge and plots a path that has a splendid ring of feasibility: of delivering net-zero emissions by around 2040. (Saul is careful not to name an actual target date, but his suggestion for your household plan for full electrification stretches to 2040.)

Saul's message is very simple and is directed to us as individuals and communities: electrify everything as and when you can. At the same time, install solar PV on rooftops, on community facilities, on top of car parks, indeed wherever you can. By his calculations this will take us to where we need to be and also be affordable.

So far, so good and no arguments. Electrification is the key driver of decarbonisation, as we can see in the Net Zero Australia (NZA) study, the results of which have just been published. But NZA also talks about gas being needed to firm up our renewable energy grid. Can both positions be right?

The NZA study is a partnership between the universities of Melbourne, Queensland and Princeton and the management consultancy Nous Group. It uses the modelling method developed by Princeton University and Evolved Energy Research for its 2020 Net-Zero America study, adapted to the boundaries of the Australian debate. NZA is rigorous and granular, evidence-driven, technology-neutral and non-political in its approach. It is the only study that has considered the totality of Australia's emissions, including those of the land sector and those associated with our exports.

In the NZA study, we considered full electrification as recommended by Saul Griffith as one scenario, and a further scenario where electrification was less rapid yet net-zero emissions was still achieved by 2050.

We can summarise the NZA results in three parts, where the words in italics represent quite different positions to those in Saul's essay:

1 To achieve an energy transformation:
   - Grow renewables as our main domestic and export energy source.
   - Install a large fleet of batteries and pumped hydro *and gas-fired power* capacity.
   - Greatly increase electrification and energy efficiency.
   - *Develop a large carbon-capture utilisation and storage industry.*
   - Greatly expand our utility networks.
   - Commit $7–9 trillion of capital investment to 2060. This excludes capital spending on the demand side: for example, vehicles and appliances; and land and agricultural sector investment.

2 To transform exports:
   - Transition to clean energy and minerals.
   - Locate export industries in the north, possibly also in the south.

3 And to invest in people, land and biodiversity:
   - Add 700,000 workers.
   - Move the land sector towards net zero.
   - Address major land-use changes.

So why have we ended up, after a very rigorous study, with some significant differences to the seemingly sensible recommendations of the Quarterly Essay? There are two answers: first, we have not forced any one favourite solution (such as renewables or nuclear) to be the main way of achieving net zero. We have forced the emission trajectory to come down to zero and then, at five-year intervals, have let a modelling package pick the cheapest supply options to meet the energy demand. This is done down to a local level and takes into consideration all manner of restrictions, be they land ownership, limitations on infrastructure on farmland, and a string of others such as biodiversity considerations, no-go areas (airports, military areas) as well as areas we want to preserve, such as inland waterways. This is a level of detail far beyond anything yet attempted for this country.

More significantly, we have considered transforming exports. Our exports of coal and LNG produce twice the emissions in the export countries as in our domestic economy. We have assumed, as others have done, that the remarkable abundance of sunlight and wind in this country will allow us to export energy, or to use this abundance to transform our existing industries such that we don't export iron ore or bauxite/alumina – rather, we will export green iron and green alumina.

On our points of difference, I would point out that, using cost projections from the CSIRO and AEMO, our calculations show that you cannot firm up the grid just with batteries and pumped hydro. You do need gas. This will be a surprise to some but we are talking decarbonised gas fed to turbines that sit around for 90+ per cent of the time doing nothing and then, on the occasions when renewables can't meet the load and we run out of pumped hydro and battery storage, kick in to keep the lights on. As well, we are talking about a bigger grid than that envisaged by Saul Griffith. We are going for net zero at home and net zero with exports.

We could cross swords on the matter of the hard-to-abate sectors, which Saul correctly lists as aviation, some aspects of freight transport, industry (for example, cement and chemicals) and agriculture. Saul's essay relies on the assumption that "the technology is on its way" to look after this sector. Our approach has been more pragmatic. On our modelling and on the work of many others, we have to build a lot, starting now. That we need three times the grid we currently have by 2030 is taken by most modellers (including AEMO) as a given. We just don't have time to wait around for new technologies, so we have used everything that is currently available. For carbon capture and storage, globally 42 Mt of CO_2 was injected in 2022, mainly for enhanced oil recovery. This is the hallmark of a developed technology, even though in Australia the rates achieved at Gorgon are nearer 2 Mt in 2022 for a project touted originally at a much higher level. We have considered that injection rates would be limited and have come out with a figure that even in the most optimistic renewables scenario, around 90 Mt per year, would be needed, because the land sector is, in our opinion, not able to supply these sorts of figures as offsets.

The NZA results and this correspondence are not a contrary view to the essay. Indeed, we would suggest that Saul Griffith is not going far enough. If Australia makes the right choices, it could grasp a once-in-a-lifetime opportunity and not only decarbonise the domestic economy but the export economy as well. It is too early to place bets on just one pathway. We need to keep a wide range of options in play, although the dominant shift to electrification cannot be avoided.

Robin Batterham

Correspondence

Heidi Lee

Since 2010, Beyond Zero Emissions has supported hundreds of energy and industry experts to crowd-source solutions that decarbonise all sectors of Australia's economy. In particular, we see an immense opportunity to establish a national network of renewable energy industrial precincts (REIPs) in our industrial heartlands. In doing this, Australia can keep pace with our trading partners, which are moving rapidly towards establishing a global green economy.

REIPs cluster manufacturers, with shared infrastructure enabling participating businesses to be powered by 100 per cent renewable energy. Our research indicates this ecosystem-level approach is the most efficient way to decarbonise our industries (which contribute almost half of Australia's domestic emissions), diversify our exports, create good, long-term jobs and unlock new economic opportunities for regional communities, such as Gladstone in Queensland and the Hunter in New South Wales.

REIPs are how Australia delivers both zero-emissions households and zero-emissions jobs, as well as replacing fossil-fuel exports with zero-emissions alternatives. As Saul Griffith writes, "Clean electric industry needs to make clean electric things for us to incorporate into our clean electric households."

Of Australia's many advantages, including critical minerals mining and renewable energy generation, perhaps the most striking is that we have recent experience in building global export industries from scratch. As recently as 2000, iron-ore exports constituted only 9 per cent ($5 billion) of Australian exports. Fast-forward to 2019 and iron ore made up more than 35 per cent of total exports, with value growing twentyfold to $100 billion.

As Beyond Zero Emissions' research shows, if we get this right, we will have developed the capability to produce the millions of machines our households and businesses need to decarbonise, our regions will thrive and we will have made the shift from significant contributor to climate change to global leader in decarbonisation without reducing our enviable living standards. That is the opportunity before us.

How do we realise this once-in-a-century opportunity? We need to rapidly build a National Supergrid that can electrify our households and our industries. We need commitment by the federal government to develop a network of REIP locations to retain and attract large industrial players and ensure our regional communities prosper. And we will need well-funded training and skills programs to retool our workforce so that it is fit for purpose in the twenty-first century.

Most importantly, we need radical collaboration. To "electrify everything," we will need leadership on all fronts: households, communities, industry and government. Local, national and international. Radical collaboration is when entire regions work together to decarbonise. With everyone coming together, Australia can become a protopia for global decarbonisation.

Heidi Lee

THE WIRES THAT BIND

Response to Correspondence

Saul Griffith

When I was at MIT Graduate School my physics and maths modelling professor, Neil Gershenfeld, was very fond of saying, "We are violently agreeing." He loved the details and it was his way of telegraphing that he was about to express a vociferous difference of opinion on some tiny detail. I too loved reading the detailed and thoughtful responses to my Quarterly Essay and find myself "violently agreeing" with most if not all of the respondents, and most but not all of their big ideas and tiny details.

Thankfully, everybody has urgency in their voices and nobody questions the climate physics. For an Australian climate debate, this is good news, a sign that we are all concerned about the lack of progress to date, and the daunting timeline of what lies ahead. David Pocock most concisely expressed this need for speed, including citing the IPCC's AR6 Synthesis Report, which didn't mince words – this is our last chance to avoid catastrophic levels of warming. Many people, and most politicians, remain ignorant of this terrible urgency. We remember the target of the IPCC's 2018 report – to halve emissions by 2050 – and so governments nominally (though not in the detail of their commitments) aim their rhetoric and policies towards that target. But that target was only possible if you started in 2018, which of course we didn't, and apart from a brief COVID-induced blip, we are emitting more than ever.

New science has also come in about the extent to which our own pollution has been masking global warming! The particulate emissions from things such as bunker fuels in ocean transport have been keeping the Earth artificially cooler than we thought. These two facts collide in my colleague Jonathan Koomey's new book *Solving Climate Change: A guide for learners and leaders*. In summary: the uncertainty about remaining carbon budgets is now larger than the actual remaining carbon budget, or in other words, our pathway to 1.5°C of warming now requires effectively zero emissions by 2040. We need more ambition and urgency, and after we inevitably move slowly for a few more years we will need even more ambition and urgency again. All of Biden's impressive climate bills do not yet put the United States on this track, not even for 2050. This is the true opportunity for Australian global leadership on climate. We can afford to do it by 2040, and if we did, we'd make it more possible for everyone else.

It is for this reason that my primary hope in the essay was to reveal, as Ian McAuley understood, "the political economy of our energy transformation and … how households have been used in the weaponisation of arguments about renewable energy." In many ways I wasn't writing this for the respondents who replied here, but to engage Australians in demanding faster action on climate. Governments don't want to go much further or more boldly than the electorate will let them, and this essay was a plea to the voters – not only can their government afford to do more, but Australia can't afford not to. I still believe we need a massively popular climate movement that is constructive and about building the future – an environmentalist movement in stark contrast to the tradition of environmentalist movements that shut things down and close the gate. We will have to create that movement, and I think our best hope is in our households, where voters live, not in boardrooms debating ESG lukewarmly.

Most respondents commented on the public appeal of electrification. My friends in climate science have been rudely ignored and even vilified. Rewiring Australia started campaigning publicly in October 2021 and we have enjoyed a huge volume of positive coverage across the media, from *The Saturday Paper* to *The Australian*, from *Nine News* to the ABC's 7.30. We are leading with a solution that everyone can understand and, in a few short years, almost everyone will be able to afford. We do not talk about abstract emissions targets or even more abstract and corruptible offsets and baselines. We talk about things everyone can have a view on: cars and stoves, solar panels and heaters, hot water and houses.

The most exciting outcome of our work is excitement itself. There is a welling up of new ideas, big bold plans and visions around the climate space such as I have not witnessed before. Communities are hosting meetings on how to increase political ambition and get their own communities to zero faster than governments are planning. The public is doing the work of governments – not everywhere, but important green shoots.

We should welcome big ideas, especially ones that are actionable today. We must go hugely fast, which should worry you, as it does Christine Milne. I find her commentary the most difficult and urgent to respond to. When we move fast we break things. The environment is already fragile from two centuries (if not two millennnia) of attack, and we should be very wary of the mistakes we could make in the next two decades. It is worth fretting over rushed permitting for nickel mines and lithium projects, and the details of where the solar and wind go. Christine (as with other respondents, notably Bjorn Sturmberg and Ian Lowe) urges reduction in demand for energy, sometimes known as efficiency.

My work has shown electrification is the principal efficiency. Electrification will likely reduce energy demand by more than 60 per cent, not only for households, but for whole nations. Electric machines and renewable generation do not squander huge amounts of energy as waste heat. Electrification is the biggest efficiency win. I'm prepared to gloss over the efficiency gains of more traditional demand reduction – using a smaller car, driving less, insulating your house, wearing a sweater – because climate solutions finally have momentum. It is now possible to fundamentally address the climate crisis without subsuming all electrical efficiency gains under a culture war over "lifestyle." I think this should be our primary strategy, but I am painfully aware that this decision glosses over the fact we should double-glaze our windows, improve building standards, build more walkable communities and drive less gigantic vehicles.

It is also true that the climate crisis is not our only ecological and planetary crisis. (As my colleague Dan Cass says, "The limits to growth is 'the most inconvenient truth.'") The biodiversity crisis could overwhelm Earth-wide systems, but before then it could quickly escalate into an urgent international food security disaster. So in this response I will be more clear, and as laconic as I can be: Electrify Everything, upgrade it when it fails, build all new things well and make everything as reusable and recyclable as is practicable. While we rush to electrify, it would be great if we could change the story about what the great suburban Australian life looks like. No more cynical and pretentious developments on the city fringe with porticoed homes of dubious quality, with multiple living spaces and levels and single-glazed windows, no insulation, several gas appliances, hot, unshaded, north-facing aspects and garages big enough for four small trucks. It really does matter whether every household has one, 1.8 or three cars. It does matter whether those cars are small or large, even if they are 100 per cent electric.

These choices made poorly will more than double the amount of material we'll need to pull from the Earth to create this future of clean machines. We absolutely should reconsider our development patterns, our architectural vernaculars, the way we have designed our schools and medical systems to embed things like extra travel and extra materials and energy into our lives. As nearly every respondent emphasised, this won't be achieved without structural and systemic change.

Christine caught me out in my own little "theory of change." Having seen no great adoption of bicycle lanes despite thirty years of agitation in this country, I've given up on the noble and the sacrificial and embraced the pragmatic – take the efficiency win of electrification and hope that as people see positive change in their communities they adopt a few other nice-to-haves, such as bicycle paths, because electric bicycles are now truly wonderful, sweat-free conveyances that flatten every hill and make every leg that of an eighteen-year-old.

Christine also puts in a very concise plea for a clean-up of our energy market bodies. The new government and new parliament have a new agenda. Their legislation was written for the age of coal and their boards were installed by a conservative government that wanted anything but clean energy progress and deep climate action. When Labor came to government it was forced to manage an energy crisis bequeathed to it by the previous government's nine years of climate war and energy ineptitude. Perhaps, now that Prime Minister Albanese has had time to reflect, there should be a review of the energy regulators which, like the Reserve Bank of Australia, must be fit-for-purpose. This would prepare for a refresh of their legislation and their boards, a flushing of the regulatory immune system. The regulators seem confused about what it will take to hit the climate target set by the IPCC in Paris: not net-zero or even real zero by 2050 – we are too slow for that; but a pathway to limit cumulative emissions as close to a 1.5°C pathway as we can get.

The current "green" plans for the National Electricity Market (NEM) are plans for climate overshoot. We still don't model the NEM ambitiously enough to account for the sector coupling that happens when we electrify all the vehicles, most of the industries and all the housing and commercial building stock.

Ian McAuley rightly points out the "imagined benefits of privatisation" of the NEM. He enthuses that energy consumer–producer households will "be participants in community renewal" and would surely agree with Heidi Lee, who writes that electrification will also have a social function in rural and regional Australia, where "entire regions work together to decarbonise."

Guilty of boostering, addicted to carrots, I have avoided the hard discussion of regulations with teeth. Perhaps my time in the Land of the Free softened me or made me frightened of things that might be conceived as infringing on personal liberty. The United States' *Inflation Reduction Act* was full of carrots – an all-incentive approach to climate action. But we won't get all the way with incentives, and many incentive-based systems are socially regressive. We must also regulate. Norway, another wealthy primary-producing country with a small population, shows us the way. They have mandated only zero-emission cars for sale by 2025. Eighty per cent of sales this year are electric. The road hasn't been perfectly smooth but they have managed it and the certainty has enabled all players to implement the policy effectively. To be very clear, it is in the interest of the energy transition to have a phase-out date for all fossil-fuelled machines, and the sooner the better. Governments are scared of the headlines around mandates and bans, but that is what is actually needed, not eventually, but soon. That means a phase-out date for gas appliances and a phase-out date for petrol and diesel vehicles that don't run on biofuels or a zero-emissions alternative. We should mandate more efficient and all-electric new construction, and even apply the same logic to major renovations. Science requires urgency and the "market" needs certainty, and the general public deserves honesty.

Rebecca Huntley rightly argues that a lot of people will need "proof of concept" of the cornucopia our all-electric protopia might provide. I can't agree more violently. It is why I have been an advocate for "pilot" projects in real communities. These shouldn't even be called pilots, but rather "proof at scale" demonstrations and social innovation incubators. Proof of the efficacy, proof of the savings, a shiny and happy community that is proof that the sky doesn't fall in when we stop putting carbon in the sky.

I have been advocating for the rapid electrification of a suburb – cars and all – for about two years now. A place in Australia, a postcode, where the future has arrived already. A place people could visit to lose their fear of the future and embrace change. Alas, fear of resentment and classic Australian cringe means these pilots will likely get watered down to less ambitious technology-testing grounds. No politician wants to be resented because they picked a winning suburb and subsidised its EVs. I get that, but the picture was much bigger, to show how it is done somewhere, including re-optimising the regulatory environment. For a very small investment in one community, the country would get an enormous discount on the decarbonisation project writ large.

So we are still embarking on this journey together, a little piecemeal. And piecemeal is a recipe for discontent, as Rebecca also points out with her crisp phrase "suburbs full of ... old tech, rising energy costs and resentment." She is right, and this is my biggest fear – for lack of the courage to show how it all works and figure out the gnarly details, we could well fail in the new culture war of who can afford to save their children's future and who can't. Better to deny the science than tell your kids you didn't have the money or unblemished credit history. The political party that figures out how to bring everyone along will have a long and vibrant popularity. It was good to see money for small businesses and social housing in the recent federal budget allocated explicitly to electrifying and efficiency. Baby steps are good. The historical moment requires leaps and bounds.

I was glad that Ian Lowe agrees that part of the climate solution is a leadership revolution which sees women taking the reins of power. Ian wants to quibble over whether an SUV that weighs twice as much causes four times as much damage or sixteen times as much damage to the road as a smaller vehicle of half the weight. I'll quickly and violently agree with him if we can use that to turn our attention urgently to the need for incentives to prevent Australia adopting even larger truckzillas – whether electric or not. Making larger vehicles pay their way is critical if we are to curb the ever-increasing size of our cars and prevent ever more of the plunder of the Earth that Christine Milne appropriately regrets.

Robin Batterham cites the Net Zero Australia (NZA) study, which produced modelling demonstrating we will have to continue to rely on gas. This research was sponsored by APA, the $22-billion gas conglomerate whose pipes carry half the nation's gas, and which owns most of the country's pipelines plus a handful of generators. I would welcome the opportunity to sit down with the authors and gas industry sponsor of the study to compare assumptions and models. As Ian Lowe said, it is "right to draw attention to the dishonest claims being made by fossil-fuel interests." One of the modellers for the NZA (America) study worked from my office for a year or so. I got to watch over her shoulder and see the inputs to their models and debate them with her. The model was flawed, and assumed one was designing the system for optimal size, not optimal cost, and hence the model didn't contemplate an over-build or over-supply of renewables with eight to twelve hours of short-term storage, something that has since been shown to be a lower-cost way of getting to a 100 per cent reliable energy system, and one that requires no gas at all. I once downloaded a handful of climate models to see whether they were all just cutting and pasting their work – I'm suspicious of models because I know how easy it is to model bullshit in and bullshit out. Those climate models turned out to be good work; the Princeton NZA modelling work was good work too, but it wasn't the last word. It would be lazy to accept the results without debate, especially in a different country and context and time with new information and new solutions. We will only get what we model and what we currently model is not ambitious enough, nor reflecting the latest and best ideas.

I also worry that Robin took the essay out of context, which was focused very much on the residential and suburban aspects of electrification, and I'd refer him to my books *The Big Switch* and *Electrify* to look at the full effects and sector coupling of the whole economy, and the likely physical and practical limits on things such as carbon capture and bio-fuels as part-solutions. These books emphasise more renewable electrification sooner for the climate targets we need.

It appears that Bjorn Sturmberg was most violently agreeing with me with his calls for rebuilding trust, collective values, reduced demand and empowering stakeholders. I couldn't agree more violently – there was a long chapter on reducing demand in the most important sector of all: transportation. There were many references to collective values being absolutely central to success on climate and charts of all the stakeholders across the energy system mapped to machines and even governance. I was precisely trying to empower stakeholders with a map, and a call to collective arms. Perhaps I didn't say enough about rebuilding trust, and I likely can't say enough. We have gutted the public sector in the past few decades. In many cases I have to buy energy data and studies that my tax dollars paid for because we farmed the work out to private enterprise. The fact we privatised energy and not water is illustrative of the plunder of the public good for private gain.

Bjorn criticises me for a lack of big ideas. I'll take that as feedback. He proposes to "provide households with a cost-free energy allowance to cover their essential needs, including refrigeration and cooking." I think this is a great idea. I have been meeting regularly with Audrey Zibelman, the former head of the Australian Energy Market Operator, to workshop exactly this idea and whether in fact we shouldn't just have a flat subscription fee for electricity, given there will be such an abundance once all the cars and batteries are connected. Unfortunately, I don't see these big ideas debated publicly and within the critical regulatory bodies. I invite Bjorn to work with me to model these things and fight the regulatory battle. We have nothing to lose except our complex bills and unfair energy contracts!

While we are at it, Bjorn, here's another big idea, and one that brings us back to Christine's concern. Each Australian currently pumps about 15 tonnes of CO_2 into the atmosphere and generates multiple tons of things like fly-ash to service their fossil-fuelled lifestyle every year. All of that is mined at great cost to the Earth. Their all-electric lifestyle will need copper, nickel, iron, lithium, silicon and other things, but these are extremely recyclable. With population declines predicted globally at the end of this century, you can squint and imagine a future with practically no more mining at the end of this century because we are recycling all the things in our energy lives. Wind turbines become more wind turbines and solar cells become more solar cells. This vision can animate us about the possibility of dedication to Christine's truly circular economy. It also emphasises that it probably isn't a great idea to rush and sell all of Australia's metal resources once, at commodity prices. Australian metals and ores are going to be electrifying every other country's machines centuries into the future. Before we sell it once and then let Korea or Japan or Germany recycle it forever, let's have a conversation about a recurring revenue business model of leasing our lithium and renting our copper with dollars perpetually flowing back into an Australian sovereign wealth fund owned by all and benefiting all rather than just a few mining magnates making a quick buck for themselves right now. If we adopt a more indigenous relationship with the land than a colonial one, where we are borrowing the land and its minerals from future generations, this transition could be the progressive opportunity of the century to share our collective natural wealth while also protecting it for those future generations.

How to do all this in the negligible time we have left? Simon Holmes à Court says we have to walk and chew gum and change everything from ballet box to switchboard at the same time – and he's right. Or as he puts it, "we need to focus on systemic change, work to build movements in our communities, elect the right people and pass the right laws." I couldn't agree more violently.

Saul Griffith

Robin Batterham is the chair of the Steering Committee of the Net Zero Australia study, a collaboration between the universities of Princeton, Melbourne and Queensland and the Nous Group. He is a former Chief Scientist of Australia.

Megan Davis is Professor of Constitutional Law at UNSW, a global Indigenous rights expert on the UN Expert Mechanism on the Rights of Indigenous Peoples, and a former chair of the UN Permanent Forum on Indigenous Issues. She was the first person to read out the Uluṟu Statement from the Heart, at Uluṟu in May 2017.

Saul Griffith is an engineer and inventor. He has been principal investigator on research projects for NASA, Advanced Research Projects Agency–Energy, the National Science Foundation and US Special Operations Command. He was awarded the MacArthur "Genius Grant" in 2007. He is a founder of the organisations Rewiring America and Rewiring Australia, and the author of *Electrify* and *The Big Switch: Australia's Electric Future.*

Simon Holmes à Court is the convenor of Climate 200, a senior adviser to the Climate and Energy College at the University of Melbourne, and director of the Smart Energy Council and the Australian Environmental Grant-makers Network.

Rebecca Huntley is one of Australia's leading social researchers. She was formerly the director of the Mind & Mood Report, Australia's longest-running social trends report, and led Vox Populi research. Her books include *Still Lucky*, *Australia Fair* and *How to Talk about Climate Change in a Way That Makes a Difference.*

Heidi Lee is CEO of Beyond Zero Emissions.

Ian Lowe is an emeritus professor of science, technology and society at Griffith University and was a reviewer for the United Nations–sponsored 2005 Millennium Assessment Report and the 2004 report of the International Geosphere-Biosphere Program. His books include *Living in the Hothouse*, *A Big Fix* and the Quarterly Essay *Reaction Time.*

Ian McAuley is a fellow of the Centre for Policy Development. He was formerly a lecturer in public finance at the University of Canberra and is now retired. In his earliest professional career, he was a power systems engineer.

Christine Milne is a former senator and was the leader of the Australian Greens from 2012 to 2015.

David Pocock is an independent senator for the ACT.

Bjorn Sturmberg is a research leader in the Battery Storage and Grid Integration Program at the ANU.

QUARTERLY ESSAY BACK ISSUES

BACK ISSUES: (Prices include GST, postage and handling within Australia.) *Grey indicates out of stock.*

- ☐ **QE 1** ($22.99) Robert Manne *In Denial*
- ☐ **QE 2** ($22.99) John Birmingham *Appeasing Jakarta*
- ☐ **QE 3** ($22.99) Guy Rundle *The Opportunist*
- ☐ **QE 4** ($22.99) Don Watson *Rabbit Syndrome*
- ☐ **QE 5** ($22.99) Mungo MacCallum *Girt By Sea*
- ☐ **QE 6** ($22.99) John Button *Beyond Belief*
- ☐ **QE 7** ($22.99) John Martinkus *Paradise Betrayed*
- ☐ **QE 8** ($22.99) Amanda Lohrey *Groundswell*
- ☐ **QE 9** ($22.99) Tim Flannery *Beautiful Lies*
- ☐ **QE 10** ($22.99) Gideon Haigh *Bad Company*
- ☐ **QE 11** ($22.99) Germaine Greer *Whitefella Jump Up*
- ☐ **QE 12** ($22.99) David Malouf *Made in England*
- ☐ **QE 13** ($22.99) Robert Manne with David Corlett *Sending Them Home*
- ☐ **QE 14** ($22.99) Paul McGeough *Mission Impossible*
- ☐ **QE 15** ($22.99) Margaret Simons *Latham's World*
- ☐ **QE 16** ($22.99) Raimond Gaita *Breach of Trust*
- ☐ **QE 17** ($22.99) John Hirst *'Kangaroo Court'*
- ☐ **QE 18** ($22.99) Gail Bell *The Worried Well*
- ☐ **QE 19** ($22.99) Judith Brett *Relaxed & Comfortable*
- ☐ **QE 20** ($22.99) John Birmingham *A Time for War*
- ☐ **QE 21** ($22.99) Clive Hamilton *What's Left?*
- ☐ **QE 22** ($22.99) Amanda Lohrey *Voting for Jesus*
- ☐ **QE 23** ($22.99) Inga Clendinnen *The History Question*
- ☐ **QE 24** ($22.99) Robyn Davidson *No Fixed Address*
- ☐ **QE 25** ($22.99) Peter Hartcher *Bipolar Nation*
- ☐ **QE 26** ($22.99) David Marr *His Master's Voice*
- ☐ **QE 27** ($22.99) Ian Lowe *Reaction Time*
- ☐ **QE 28** ($22.99) Judith Brett *Exit Right*
- ☐ **QE 29** ($22.99) Anne Manne *Love & Money*
- ☐ **QE 30** ($22.99) Paul Toohey *Last Drinks*
- ☐ **QE 31** ($22.99) Tim Flannery *Now or Never*
- ☐ **QE 32** ($22.99) Kate Jennings *American Revolution*
- ☐ **QE 33** ($22.99) Guy Pearse *Quarry Vision*
- ☐ **QE 34** ($22.99) Annabel Crabb *Stop at Nothing*
- ☐ **QE 35** ($22.99) Noel Pearson *Radical Hope*
- ☐ **QE 36** ($22.99) Mungo MacCallum *Australian Story*
- ☐ **QE 37** ($22.99) Waleed Aly *What's Right?*
- ☐ **QE 38** ($22.99) David Marr *Power Trip*
- ☐ **QE 39** ($22.99) Hugh White *Power Shift*
- ☐ **QE 40** ($22.99) George Megalogenis *Trivial Pursuit*
- ☐ **QE 41** ($22.99) David Malouf *The Happy Life*
- ☐ **QE 42** ($22.99) Judith Brett *Fair Share*
- ☐ **QE 43** ($22.99) Robert Manne *Bad News*
- ☐ **QE 44** ($22.99) Andrew Charlton *Man-Made World*
- ☐ **QE 45** ($22.99) Anna Krien *Us and Them*
- ☐ **QE 46** ($22.99) Laura Tingle *Great Expectations*
- ☐ **QE 47** ($22.99) David Marr *Political Animal*
- ☐ **QE 48** ($22.99) Tim Flannery *After the Future*
- ☐ **QE 49** ($22.99) Mark Latham *Not Dead Yet*
- ☐ **QE 50** ($22.99) Anna Goldsworthy *Unfinished Business*
- ☐ **QE 51** ($22.99) David Marr *The Prince*
- ☐ **QE 52** ($22.99) Linda Jaivin *Found in Translation*
- ☐ **QE 53** ($22.99) Paul Toohey *That Sinking Feeling*
- ☐ **QE 54** ($22.99) Andrew Charlton *Dragon's Tail*
- ☐ **QE 55** ($22.99) Noel Pearson *A Rightful Place*
- ☐ **QE 56** ($22.99) Guy Rundle *Clivosaurus*
- ☐ **QE 57** ($22.99) Karen Hitchcock *Dear Life*
- ☐ **QE 58** ($22.99) David Kilcullen *Blood Year*
- ☐ **QE 59** ($22.99) David Marr *Faction Man*
- ☐ **QE 60** ($22.99) Laura Tingle *Political Amnesia*
- ☐ **QE 61** ($22.99) George Megalogenis *Balancing Act*
- ☐ **QE 62** ($22.99) James Brown *Firing Line*
- ☐ **QE 63** ($22.99) Don Watson *Enemy Within*
- ☐ **QE 64** ($22.99) Stan Grant *The Australian Dream*
- ☐ **QE 65** ($22.99) David Marr *The White Queen*
- ☐ **QE 66** ($22.99) Anna Krien *The Long Goodbye*
- ☐ **QE 67** ($22.99) Benjamin Law *Moral Panic 101*
- ☐ **QE 68** ($22.99) Hugh White *Without America*
- ☐ **QE 69** ($22.99) Mark McKenna *Moment of Truth*
- ☐ **QE 70** ($22.99) Richard Denniss *Dead Right*
- ☐ **QE 71** ($22.99) Laura Tingle *Follow the Leader*
- ☐ **QE 72** ($22.99) Sebastian Smee *Net Loss*
- ☐ **QE 73** ($22.99) Rebecca Huntley *Australia Fair*
- ☐ **QE 74** ($22.99) Erik Jensen *The Prosperity Gospel*
- ☐ **QE 75** ($22.99) Annabel Crabb *Men at Work*
- ☐ **QE 76** ($22.99) Peter Hartcher *Red Flag*
- ☐ **QE 77** ($22.99) Margaret Simons *Cry Me a River*
- ☐ **QE 78** ($22.99) Judith Brett *The Coal Curse*
- ☐ **QE 79** ($22.99) Katharine Murphy *The End of Certainty*
- ☐ **QE 80** ($22.99) Laura Tingle *The High Road*
- ☐ **QE 81** ($22.99) Alan Finkel *Getting to Zero*
- ☐ **QE 82** ($22.99) George Megalogenis *Exit Strategy*
- ☐ **QE 83** ($22.99) Lech Blaine *Top Blokes*
- ☐ **QE 84** ($22.99) Jess Hill *The Reckoning*
- ☐ **QE 85** ($22.99) Sarah Krasnostein *Not Waving, Drowning*
- ☐ **QE 86** ($27.99) Hugh White *Sleepwalk to War*
- ☐ **QE 87** ($27.99) Waleed Aly & Scott Stephens *Uncivil Wars*
- ☐ **QE 88** ($27.99) Katharine Murphy *Lone Wolf*
- ☐ **QE 89** ($27.99) Saul Griffith *The Wires That Bind*

Please include this form with delivery and payment details overleaf.
Back issues also available as eBooks at **quarterlyessay.com**

SUBSCRIBE TO RECEIVE 10% OFF THE COVER PRICE

☐ **ONE-YEAR PRINT AND DIGITAL SUBSCRIPTION: $89.99**

- Print edition
- Home delivery
- Automatically renewing
- Full digital access to all past issues
- App for Android and iPhone users
- eBook files

DELIVERY AND PAYMENT DETAILS

DELIVERY DETAILS:

NAME:

ADDRESS:

EMAIL: PHONE:

PAYMENT DETAILS: Enclose a cheque/money order made out to Schwartz Books Pty Ltd.
Or debit my credit card (MasterCard, Visa and Amex accepted).
Freepost: Quarterly Essay, Reply Paid 90094, Collingwood VIC 3066
All prices include GST, postage and handling.

CARD NO. ☐☐☐☐☐☐☐☐☐☐☐☐☐☐☐☐

EXPIRY DATE: / CCV: AMOUNT: $

PURCHASER'S NAME: SIGNATURE:

Subscribe online at **quarterlyessay.com/subscribe** • Freecall: 1800 077 514 • Phone: 03 9486 0288
Email: subscribe@quarterlyessay.com (please do not send electronic scans of this form)